Deepening the Colors

DEEPENING THE COLORS

Life inside the story of God

Syd Hielema

DORDT COLLEGE PRESS

Cover design by Scott Vande Kraats
Cover art by Matt Kunnari
Illustrations by Sarah (Versluis) De Young

Dordt College Press   www.dordt.edu/DCPcatalog
498 Fourth Avenue NE
Sioux Center, Iowa 51250
United States of America

ISBN: 978-1-940567-11-2

Printed in the United States of America

The Library of Congress Cataloguing-in-Publication Date is on files with the Library of Congress, Washington D.C.

Library of Congress Control Number: 2014951430

Prelude

It still seemed to be early, and the morning freshness was in the air. They kept on stopping to look around and to look behind them, partly because it was so beautiful but partly also because there was something about it which they could not understand.

"Peter," said Lucy, "where is this, do you suppose?"

"I don't know," said the High King, "It reminds me of somewhere but I can't give it a name. Could it be somewhere we once stayed for a holiday when we were very, very small?"

"It would have to have been a jolly good holiday," said Eustace. "I bet there isn't a country like this anywhere in our world. Look at the colors! You couldn't get a blue like the blue on those mountains in our world."

"Is it not Aslan's country?" said Tirian.

"Not like Aslan's country on top of that mountain beyond the Eastern end of the world," said Jill. "I've been there."

"If you ask me," said Edmund, "it's like somewhere in the Narnian world. Look at those mountains ahead—and the big ice-mountains beyond them. Surely they're rather like the mountains we used to see from Narnia, the ones up Westward beyond the Waterfall?"

"Yes, so they are," said Peter. "Only these are bigger."

"I don't think *those* ones are so very like anything in Narnia," said Lucy. "But look there." She pointed Southward to their left, and everyone stopped and turned to look. "Those hills," said Lucy, "the nice woody ones and the blue ones behind—aren't they very like the Southern border of Narnia?"

"Like!" cried Edmund after a moment's silence. "Why, they're exactly like. Look, there's Mount Pire with his forked head, and there's the pass into Archenland and everything!"

"And yet they're not like," said Lucy. "They're different. They have more colors on them and they look further away than I remember and they're more . . . more . . . oh, I don't know. . . ."

"More like the real thing," said Lord Digory softly.

From *The Last Battle,* C. S. Lewis, pp. 209f. (HarperTrophy edition)

Table of Contents

Chapter One

Recognizing the King

> Once, having been asked by the Pharisees when the kingdom of God would come, Jesus replied, "The kingdom of God does not come with your careful observation, nor will people say, 'Here it is,' or 'There it is,' because the kingdom of God is within you." (Luke 17:20–21)

What did he say? "The kingdom of God is within you?" What's that supposed to mean?

Oh, that man is so slippery, so confusing. Every week we sit down with each other and ask the same questions, "How can we trap that man? What question can we ask him in public that will expose him as a fraud, an unfaithful Jew, a rebel against Rome? How can we get him arrested or, at the very least, discredited?" And every week the same pattern continues: we find the "perfect" question, we find the "perfect" time to pose it to him in public, and he turns the tables on us, embarrasses us, confuses us.

We, the members of the ruling Sanhedrin, had thought today's question was foolproof. He's always talking about the kingdom, and the people are eager to hear more, wondering if he will be the king that will free our land once again. But he always talks in parables, in riddles, as though he's trying to hide something, tantalizing the crowds with word pictures that are ambiguous and evocative. So we said to each other, "Enough of this wordplay. Let's pin him down with a direct question: "When will the kingdom of God come?" If he says that he doesn't know or that it could take many centuries, the crowds will see him for the fraud he really is and turn against him. And if he says, 'It's almost here—any day now you will see it come,' we will report his words directly to Pontius Pilate as the words of one inciting insurrection against the Roman authorities."

But what did he say? "The kingdom of God is within you." What is that supposed to mean? Is this kingdom here now? Within me? Within all of these people, including this rabble that hangs on his every word? Where? In my heart? Is there a king ruling in my heart? How can a kingdom be inside me while we are under Roman occupation?

These thoughts get us nowhere. The man is a blasphemer who needs to be put away before he causes so much trouble that the Roman armies come and massacre us all. What question can we ask him next?

****

Confused by Jesus. Has it ever happened to you? It's one of the most important ways in which Jesus deepens your colors.

If you've never been confused by Jesus, the odds are you've never taken him seriously. The four gospels of Matthew, Mark, Luke, and John consistently portray Jesus as a Savior who left dumbfounded perplexity and amazement in his wake everywhere that he went. At age twelve, he baffled the scholars in the temple (Luke 2), and during his adult ministry, he confounded almost everyone whose path he crossed. We read that because of his teaching "all his opponents were humiliated" (Luke 13:17), that after he stilled the storm his disciples cried out in fear and amazement, "Who is this? He commands even the winds and the water and they obey him" (Luke 8:25), and that "the crowds were amazed at his teaching, because he taught as one who had authority, and not as their teachers of the law" (Matthew 7:28–29).

The purpose of this book is to explore questions like, "What is my place in God's world?" and "What am I called to do and be, and how do I know?" These questions often take us through fogs of confusion, and they also drive us to our knees. But Jesus does not usually answer our prayers with a great light that instantly melts away our fog. His way tends to respond to our questions with more questions, deeper questions, questions that expand our range of vision as though he is taking us up in an airplane to help us see the bigger picture, the bigger questions. The question "What is my place in God's world?" is a bit like asking, "How does the one piece of the jigsaw puzzle that is my life fit into this multimillioned piece picture?" To process that question, we need to know the shape and color of our particular piece and we need some sense of the entire picture.

Deepening the Colors will describe that bigger picture before arriving at the "What am I called to do?" question in its last chapter. Along the way, we will explore what it means to grow to maturity in Christ, how this maturity relates to God's original intentions for humankind (before the fall into sin) as creatures made in his image, and how our callings fit inside the coming of the kingdom of God.

Matthew tells us that when Jesus began his ministry, his message could be summed up in one short sentence: "Repent, for the kingdom of heaven is near" (Matthew 4:17). The word *kingdom* occurs 115 times in the four gospels and is more central to Jesus's teaching and person than any other concept or principle. The prayer that Jesus taught his disciples to pray includes that short but powerful petition, "Thy kingdom come, thy will be done on earth as it is in heaven" (Matthew 6:10), which is both a request for the Lord to reveal his ruling power on earth and a commitment by the one praying to "seek first the kingdom" (Matthew 6:33). The gospels make it clear that if we have anything to do with Jesus of Nazareth, we must come to terms with his claim that he is the king of a kingdom, and—as our Pharisee friend learned—that kingdom is within us.

The Kingdom of God

I once heard a believer say, "When I was fifteen, I surrendered my life to Jesus my Savior, but it took me twenty years to realize that he was also the Lord over all." The Bible talks more about Jesus as the sovereign Lord than as our Savior (though he is both), but we tend to focus on him as our Savior because it's *easier.* Someone who forgives our sins and then gives us eternal life, well, that sounds wonderful! But when he also says, "I am now the Lord of your life; submit every single part of your being to me as your Lord," it starts to sound a little threatening. Paul sums up this lordship claim very succinctly in his teaching: "Whatever you do, whether in word or in deed, do it all in the name of the Lord Jesus, giving thanks to God the Father through him" (Colossians 3:17). That's *kingdom* language. That's putting into practice Jesus's claim that "all authority in heaven and on earth has been given to me" (Matthew 28:18). I am not just saved; I am *owned* by the King who is Lord over all. Or, as one famous confession puts it, my only comfort is "that I am not my own, but belong—body and soul, in life and in death—to my faithful Savior Jesus Christ" (Heidelberg Catechism, Lord's Day 1).

If you are a Christian, do you walk with the one who is both your Savior and your Lord, or do you tend to emphasize the first part more than the second? Jesus both deals with sin and rules over a kingdom, or, to put it more accurately, dealing with sin is a major way in which Jesus rules over the kingdom. I have been a teacher and preacher of the Bible for many years, but I still struggle with explaining clearly what the Scriptures have to say about the kingdom. Because kingdom realities are bigger than the human intellect, I share some of the confusions of our Pharisee friend at the beginning of this chapter. The best I can do is to summarize the Bible's teachings in these summary statements.

1. The kingdom of God declares God's rule over the entire universe.

Imagine God the creator looking over his finished creation at the end of Genesis 1: "God saw all that he had made, and it was very good" (Genesis 1:31). The picture is a kingly one: the king is inspecting his newly created kingdom and declares that it is wonderful. The Bible opens with a kingdom vision in Genesis 1, and this vision continues right through to the closing chapters of Revelation. This kingdom vision goes through many twists and turns from the Bible's beginning to the end, but God is always the one in charge, the ruler on the throne, the sovereign Lord over all. "The earth is the Lord's and everything in it, the world, and all who live in it" (Psalm 24:1).

The Lord has given Jesus authority over all things (Matthew 28:18), and in Jesus "God is reconciling all things to himself" (Colossians 1:20). *Reconciling* means "restoring shalom," that is, restoring the complete harmony that was meant to be between all creatures and God. We might call the kingdom God's "grand universe-reclamation project." Our lives reflect that project, too, as we "shine like stars in the universe" and "hold out the word of life" (Philippians 2:15–16).

2. The kingdom is here and it is coming.

Imagine yourself living with Jesus after he returns. The unique person that you are now will be purified, and "you" will be more "yourself" than you have ever been before. God is making you new now, but his current work is like a tiny beginning that "he will bring to completion" (Philippians 1:6). As we are aware of these tiny beginnings, we can extrapolate from them to imagine, just a little, what we might be like as finished new creations. When I glimpse the wonder of love in another person, I can imagine the beauty of seeing her overflowing with that love. But the kingdom is not just about human beings. The entire *creation* will be more fully "itself" than it has ever been. Isaiah pictures that "the wolf will live with the lamb, the leopard will lie down with the goat . . . for the earth will be full of the knowledge of the Lord" (Isaiah 11:6, 9). We are part of a kingdom that is "on the way"; God rules over it now, guiding it to its completion, its perfection.

Christians often speak of "the now and the not yet" of the kingdom. In many ways, the kingdom is like a fetus: it exists, it is a definite reality, and yet it is hidden, still growing, invisible in many ways, sensed by the occasional kick and a swelling belly. Romans 8 describes one of the most profound pictures of the kingdom here and coming as it speaks of both believers and the entire creation groaning as if in the pains of childbirth, waiting for the glory of the Lord to be revealed (vv. 22–23). The kingdom has come; Jesus is Lord already. But his lordship is intensely challenged, leading believers to groan in longing for the battle to be done and the kingdom to be fully revealed.

3. Currently God's rule is contested.

Spiritual warfare: it's everywhere. Spiritual warfare refers to kingdoms in conflict. Yes, the kingdom is within you and me, but because of its presence, a battle rages within us. The devil seeks to contest the lordship of Jesus in any way that he can: seducing humankind with the illusion of power and might; promoting idolatries and immoralities; celebrating the spread of disease and abuse; making hopelessness, discouragement, and violence contagious; using heresies and distortions to masquerade as God's own truth. This shows up in our own lives and in society in hundreds of different ways, from my desires to control other people and use them as means to my ends to government regulations that favor the powerful and wealthy. Frequently the power of evil *seems* much stronger than the lordship of Jesus because God's strength is particularly revealed in weakness, epitomized by a Lord dying on a cross. Asserting the lordship of Christ and acknowledging his authority in an evil world is an act of faith expressed in the words of that beautiful hymn: "For though the wrong seems oft so strong, God is the ruler yet" ("This Is My Father's World," v. 2).

Sometimes Christians speak of spiritual warfare as a phenomenon limited to conflicts between demons and angels in which human beings find themselves caught up. This understanding of spiritual warfare reflects a compartmentalized understanding of the Christian faith that severely limits its scope. Spiritual warfare *does* involve demons and angels, but it also involves my decisions, human sickness and health, economic policies, how people worship, the actions of governments, how I manage my time. Because God's kingdom rule covers everything that exists, spiritual warfare also involves absolutely everything. The hours I spend playing video games, the choices I make in spending my money, the conversations I have with others—they all occur on the battlefield; each one involves a struggle between the kingdom of God and the challenges to that kingdom.

Because God's rule is contested, life in the kingdom always involves suffering. Battlefields are filled with casualties, and some people are more wounded than others. One sixteen-year-old dies of cancer while another struggles with loneliness. Kingdom life involves both seeing and responding to the suffering around us and within us. In one of Jesus's final parables, he describes the judgment that separates the sheep from the goats (Matthew 25:31–48). What's the main difference between the two? The sheep fed the hungry, clothed the naked, visited the sick, and invited the strangers in.

They saw that in a world in which God's rule is contested, they were called to minister to those who were suffering.

4. We are called to pray for the kingdom and to work toward its coming.

There are two central commands of Jesus that relate to the kingdom, and both are found in Matthew 6. In the Lord's Prayer, Jesus teaches us to pray, "Thy kingdom come" (v. 10). Later, acknowledging that we often become preoccupied with immediate needs, such as food and clothing, he concludes, "The pagans run after all these things, and your heavenly Father knows that you need them. But seek first his kingdom and his righteousness, and all these things will be added to you as well" (vv. 32–33). These two commands embody the beautiful paradox of partnership with God. On the one hand, we are called to *pray* for the kingdom to come, to be brought to completion. On the other hand, such prayer does not allow us to be passive and "watch on the sidelines" as the Lord gets it done. Rather, he uses us in the coming of the kingdom; we are called to seek it first, to make it our number one priority, to place our entire lives under the heading of "seeking first the kingdom." We are called to be God's partners in his grand universe-reclamation project by both praying and working for the kingdom.

This "partnership paradox" can be traced all the way back to Genesis 1. God the king scans the wonders of his creation-kingdom and declares it to be very good, and he also creates humankind in his image so that they will rule over his creation. Even after sin infects humankind, God still walks with us as his kingdom partners, leading David to exclaim, "You have made [humankind] a little lower than the heavenly beings, and crowned him with glory and honor. You made him ruler over the works of your hands; you put everything under his feet" (Psalm 8:5–6).

5. We are called to abandon everything for the kingdom; we are called to embrace everything within the kingdom.

Matthew 13 contains the greatest concentration of Jesus's kingdom teachings. There we find another paradox. On the one hand, "The kingdom of heaven is like a treasure hidden in a field. When a man found it, he hid it again and then in his joy went and sold all he had and bought that field" (v. 44). We are called to abandon everything else for the sake of the kingdom. Nothing else matters anymore because it all pales in contrast with its treasure. In the gospels, Jesus teaches us that nothing—including family, daily work, possessions, and even religious rituals—may take priority over the kingdom. All must be abandoned for him. In a culture that preaches *entitlement*—"you deserve your rights and make sure you get what's coming to you"—kingdom abandonment is very difficult to live out.

But, because of the kingdom, everything else matters even more than it did before! Everything in our lives is "infected" with the "kingdom virus." "The kingdom of heaven is like yeast that a woman took and mixed into a large amount of flour until it worked through the dough" (v. 33). This treasure for which everything else was abandoned is also like yeast, which infiltrates everything and transforms it from flat, lifeless dough into risen, nourishing, delicious bread. The yeast dissolves and becomes invisible except that its presence is seen in its effects. The whole is transformed because the power of the kingdom is alive within it. Nineteenth-century German pastor Christoph Blumhardt speaks of the double conversion of the Christian. First, the Christian is converted away from the world to focus entirely on Christ and his kingdom. Then, in the name of Jesus, the Christian is converted back to the world to claim it all in his name. This double conversion captures something of the paradox of the treasure and the yeast, the paradox of abandoning all for the kingdom and embracing all in the name of the King. Because the kingdom is my treasure, I am called to abandon my friends. Because the kingdom is a yeast, I am called to reclaim my friends, bringing Spirit-yeast to my friendships so that these relationships further the coming of the kingdom.

Occasionally a student walks into my office and says something like, "My girlfriend is so important to me, I'm afraid that she means more to me than Jesus does. Do you think we should break up?" I've never encouraged ending such a relationship, but the question illustrates the abandon/embrace kingdom principle. If my girlfriend is more important to me than Jesus, then we don't have a kingdom relationship. But if I abandon her as the *center* of my life and then embrace her again as a *partner* in seeking first the kingdom, our priorities make more sense.

6. We can see glimpses of the kingdom coming in many places, but we cannot find any perfect embodiments of the kingdom.

Seeing the kingdom as it comes takes a special kind of vision; it takes what we might call "born-again eyes." As Jesus said to Nicodemus in their late-night conversation, "I tell you the truth, no one can see the kingdom of God unless he is born again" (John 3:3). We've all had the experience of leaving the bright outdoors and entering a room that is totally dark. At first, our eyes can see only blackness everywhere, but after a time, our eyes adjust and we begin to recognize shapes and outlines within the darkened room. Seeing the coming kingdom is somewhat like that: our eyes grow to see things that we couldn't see at first, and our seeing grows in two ways: we see the kingdom coming in many places, and we see that there are no perfect embodiments of the kingdom.

First, we see the kingdom coming in many (even unlikely) places. For example, I see the kingdom coming in the two *Shrek* movies. We live in a culture obsessed with personal appearance, and there are voices all around us broadcasting night and day the message "you are what you look like." The *Shrek* movies poke

fun at this lie by rejecting cultural definitions of beauty and celebrating instead deeper human qualities. I do not know if any of
the movies' producers and writers are Christians, but I do know
that their message resonates with the biblical declaration that
"man looks at the outward appearance but the Lord looks at the
heart" (1 Samuel 16:7).

Second, because the kingdom is both here and still coming,
we cannot find any perfect embodiments of it in this world.
There are Christians who act as though their particular nation,
political party, denomination, Christian organization or ministry, family, or even their own opinions are to be treated as perfect embodiments of the kingdom and must not be criticized or
subjected to scrutiny in any way. Such behavior is very dangerous and actually undermines the coming of the kingdom in two
ways: first, by claiming to accurately embody the kingdom, it
assumes that this perfect embodiment cannot be improved, and
therefore its current imperfections will never be challenged to
change. Second, it fosters a spiritual pride that creates division
among Christians; if my "kingdom embodiment" is perfect,
than yours is inevitably inferior, and it makes no sense for us to
work together.

The kingdom of God involves much more than these six
statements can describe, but these six give us a good start for
living under the lordship of Jesus Christ. My piece of the jigsaw
puzzle is a kingdom piece, and because the entire puzzle picture
shows me the kingdom that is here and also coming, finding my
place in God's world is a kingdom question. The greatest guide
for working on this jigsaw puzzle is God's holy word, the Bible;
I also need to understand how the Bible helps me to see the
kingdom picture and my place in it.

The Kingdom Inside the Story of God

Have you ever used the "search-engine" approach to seeking guidance from the Bible? It's quite simple: you punch in the particular issue or problem that you need guidance for, click on "Go," and the computer pulls up the verses that you need to read to solve your problem. Is your problem stress? Punch it in, and up come many passages, including Psalm 23:2: "He makes me lie down in green pastures, He leads me beside quiet waters." After reading this verse and the many others my computer has pointed me to, I hope that my anxiety will be relieved.

The search-engine approach might be helpful occasionally, but the Bible was not primarily written to solve my problems. Its main purpose is to reveal the Lord God to us, so that in coming to know him we come to know who we are and how we live in his world. This kind of knowledge isn't something that we are given in its totality. Instead, it's a knowing that we gradually deepen over the course of many years of living with the book, in the same way that a husband gradually comes to know his wife more and more fully during many years of marriage. As we read and live the story of God—the story of the King who is faithful to his kingdom—the picture becomes richer and more vibrant, the colors become deeper. And as the book leads us to deepen the colors of our understanding of God, the colors of our own lives become deeper as we follow him.

It works like this. One of the Bible's pictures of the fullness of the kingdom of God is found in Revelation 21, where John describes this vision:

> Then I saw a new heaven and a new earth, for the first heaven and the first earth had passed away, and there was no longer any sea. I saw the Holy City, the new Jerusalem, coming down out of heaven from God. . . . The wall was made of jasper, and the city of pure gold, as pure as glass. The foundations of the city walls were decorated with every kind of precious stone. The first foundation was jasper, the second sapphire,

the third chalcedony, the fourth emerald, the fifth sardonyx, the sixth carnelian, the seventh chrysolite, the eighth beryl, the ninth topaz, the tenth chrysoprase, the eleventh jacinth, and the twelfth amethyst. The twelve gates were made of twelve pearls, each gate made of a single pearl. The great street of the city was of pure gold, like transparent glass. (Revelation 21:1–2, 18–21)

Why does John take such care to name each individual jewel that he sees in the Holy City? In our world, we associate jewels with riches, but in John's world, jewels were associated with intense colors as light shone on them and through them. The completed kingdom is a place of multicolored richness, intense shining that sparkles with the glory of God. The New Jerusalem glows with the deepest emerald greens and pearl whites. That's where the story of God reaches its final climax.

But those colors don't just show up at the end like a prize that everyone has been waiting for. We can trace those colors all the way through the entire book. You might say that the Bible is like a six-chapter storybook that could be subtitled "the story of God deepening the colors." It begins (as it ends) in the first chapter with a rich intensity of color, but its beginning is the multicolored splash of a garden instead of a city. A man and a woman are created in God's image to rule over his garden, to enjoy its colors and to serve them so that they shine more brightly. We see the colors of *shalom,* everything that exists in complete harmony with its Creator and with all other creatures. But in the second chapter of this story, a serpent persuades this man and woman to fall into sin, and all of the colors are distorted. They blur together, dark blotches stain them everywhere, and the original shalom is lost.

The story reveals that God is, at heart, a faithful promise-keeper, and he promises that the colors will be restored; from Genesis 3 onward, the Bible is the story of God holding on to those perverted colors and leading them on the way to their renewal, to their fullest deepening. Early on he gives Noah and his family a rainbow as a sign of his faithfulness, as if to say, "Look in the sky and remember that colorful shalom is on the way back." The third chapter of the story of God is the account of God's promise that he will deal with sin; he will be faithful, and he calls his people to be faithful to him as well. Throughout much of the Old Testament, the temple is the clearest symbol to God's people that he is with them—a building filled with multi-colored precious stones and jewels, a foretaste of the New Jerusalem John saw in Revelation 21.

In the fourth chapter, the promised deliverer comes, Jesus Christ, the king of the kingdom, the redeemer of the world. He is the fullness of God's colors; he is a living rainbow; he is complete shalom in human flesh; he is the true temple. But the sinful, color-distorted world rejected the son of God and put him to death. However, God raised him up and declared that his color-deepening project could not be stopped. Through the resurrected Jesus, God says, "The new creation is on the way. I have conquered sin and death and will share this new life with you."

We live in the fifth chapter of the story of God, the chapter that occurs between the two comings of Jesus Christ. This chapter begins with the sending of the Holy Spirit on Pentecost Sunday (Acts 2), the Spirit that is contagious with the colors of Jesus, spreading them to all who surrender their lives to him. The colors that were in that Old Testament temple and then taken over by Jesus are now in us: "Don't you know that you are God's temple and that God's Spirit lives in you?" (1 Corinthians 3:16). To be a Christian is to look back to see the multicolored shalom of Jesus, to look ahead the see the multicolored shalom of the entire universe made new, and to know that in between these two "rainbows," the Holy Spirit is transforming us, deepening our colors little by little. Paul puts it this way: "We, who with unveiled faces all reflect the Lord's glory, are being transformed into his likeness with ever-increasing glory, which comes from the Lord, who is the Spirit" (2 Corinthians 3:18). Think of all of the questions that verse raises: What does "ever-increasing glory" look like? How often do you describe your life with that phrase? What does it mean to find our places in the kingdom of God as people who "are being transformed into his likeness?" What does our daily life look like as we are so transformed? Those are the questions this book will probe, questions that explore what a life of deepening our colors with Jesus looks like.

Our colors are being deepened now, on the way to the sixth chapter, the final transformation of all things. When the end of all things arrives, the wolf will lie down with the lamb; sickness and crying and pain will be banished forever; and every tint, shade, hue, and tone that exists in the entire universe will shine with the glory of God, singing out the shalom that will never end.

The story of God

First chapter   The world is created (Genesis 1–2).
Second chapter   The world falls into sin (Genesis 3:1–7).
Third chapter   A savior is promised (Genesis 3:8–Malachi).
Fourth chapter   The savior comes (Matthew–Acts 1).
Fifth chapter   The Holy Spirit is poured out (Acts 2–Revelation 20).
Sixth chapter   The new creation comes (Revelation 21–22).

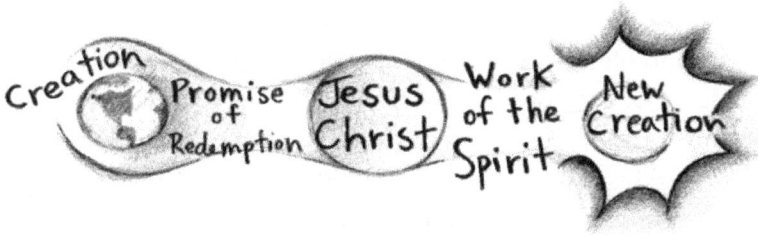

Creation — Promise of Redemption — Jesus Christ — Work of the Spirit — New Creation

Following Jesus Inside the "Bowtie"

Another way to describe the relationship between Jesus and the kingdom of God is by means of the bowtie diagram seen below. A bowtie is really a ribbon that is tied in a certain way in the center to hold the shape of a bow. God's works of creation and redemption are like a ribbon that is held together by Jesus Christ in the following way.

The left edge is the creation of the universe, all of reality held in the hands of God. This world fell into sin; at that point, the Lord promises redemption, and the entire Old Testament is "pregnant with Jesus," as it were. Thousands of events, relationships, promises, and so on are all leading up to one very specific event: the birth of a baby in a manger in Bethlehem.

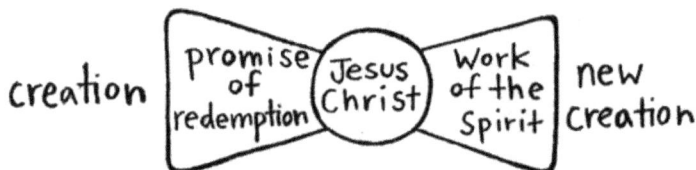

At the center of the bowtie stand the birth, life, death, resurrection, and ascension of Jesus Christ. He brings to fulfillment everything before him, and all that happens after him flows from his life. He shows us what God's creation and redemption are all about, walking as a man of shalom in a very broken and needy world, bringing in the kingdom of God. But then he ascended to heaven, and by all appearances, the earth looked as though nothing had changed at all, except that there were fewer lepers and blind folks and several angry Pharisees.

But his ascension was in fact his way of spreading his shalom-contagious life. "You will do greater things than these," he says to his disciples, meaning, you will receive the Holy Spirit, my Spirit, and in the power of the Spirit, you will also become contagious with shalom, kingdom-seekers who spread the gospel to the ends of the earth: "I tell you the truth, it is for your good that I am going away. Unless I go away, the counselor will not come to you; but if I go, I will send him to you" (John 16:7). After the ascension and the sending of that promised counselor at Pentecost, we see the bowtie expanding outward again—until it reaches its right edge, the fullness of the new creation when Jesus returns and everything is made new again. The right half of the bowtie—the half that describes where we live—can also be called *the coming of the kingdom*. The bowtie helps us to understand what is involved in discerning God's call to us.

One day a young woman went to Jesus and asked, "Master, what must I do? What is my calling in life?"

Jesus looked at her and saw the earnestness in her eyes. "Follow me," he replied, "and you will have treasure in heaven."

"I will," she replied eagerly. "Though I have just begun another year of schooling, I will put away my bags and my books and follow you."

"I did not ask you to put them away," said Jesus, "I simply called you to follow me."

Her glowing eyes turned to anxious confusion. "But you are here and my schooling is over there; I must follow you where you are."

He smiled, "I am here, *and* I am there. Find me there and follow me; seek first the kingdom."

"I see you now—here. How can I see you there?"

"I *am* there. Seek and you will find, be patient, persevere."

"But where will you lead me?"

He was silent for a moment as he gazed into her eyes. "Follow, and you will see. To places that are good but also difficult. To tasks that are clear but also confusing. To people who are loving but also selfish. To roads that are straight but also treacherous. Follow, and you will never be alone."

She nodded and went away, pondering these words in her heart, not sure whether she was joyful or sad or both. "I will seek you," she prayed, "open my eyes that I may see."

****

Finding our place in the story of God is a "Follow him" journey that participates in this process of deepening or intensifying the colors of our lives. This book is an invitation to *examine* the colors of your own life as the light of Jesus shines on them, and to seek the *deepening* of these colors through following where Jesus leads. Historians have noted that during the seventy years of Soviet (Russian) communism, individuals became faceless "comrades" dressed in grey; personal identity became irrelevant before the grand cause of the communist state. The kingdom of God is just the opposite: on the way toward its grandeur, every person who surrenders as a slave of Christ becomes more "face-full," more fully him or herself, more colorful. My prayer is that you will enjoy the deepening colors the Lord is painting within you as you walk through the pages ahead.

Chapter Two

I Am a CALLED Person

The God Who Calls

When I entered college in 1972, I had only two relatively clear thoughts concerning a career path: my dream was to earn a living by composing music, and I was absolutely certain that I would never become a teacher. During the past three decades, I have spent most of my working hours in front of a classroom and have occasionally composed a piece that was sung by the church choir or congregation. How could I have been so wrong on both counts? What would lead the eighteen-year-old me to declare so vehemently that teaching was out of the question when I have found so much joy in it for thirty years?

It's very common for Christians to struggle about their calling in life. "What am I supposed to do?" we wonder. "What is God calling me to? Should I take over the family farm or go into agricultural engineering? Should I seek to get married soon or wait a few years? I'm a people person: am I more suited to social work or nursing or teaching? I have a passion for issues related to politics and justice, but are there any realistic careers that flow from that passion? I have some questions about the denomination that I was raised in. Should I explore joining another church? Now that my children have reached adulthood, should we move closer to my aging parents?" Questions such as these are crucial, and we need to struggle through them. Some of these questions may be resolved quite easily; others may involve years of ambivalence before we come to a fairly clear conclusion—or they may never be fully resolved. Along the way, many of us experience a great deal of anxiety about such questions.

When we ask ourselves what we are supposed to do in specific areas of our lives, we are asking a "God question." Whenever we ask "God questions," we need to step back and ask "what assumptions about God am I making when I ask these questions? Why does God call me to do anything at all?" Most of us have used a camera or a camcorder that has a zoom lens. The question "What am I supposed to do?" is like a camera whose zoom lens is focused on the smallest picture possible. If we can put our finger on the zoom button, the picture expands and our question becomes, "Who am I called *to be*? What kind of a *person* is God shaping in me?" Continuing expansion of the zoom lens allows us to hear the question, "Who does God call the *Christian community* to be? How is God's shaping of me part of his forming an entire *body* of people?" Finally, with the camera focused on the biggest picture possible, we hear the question, "How does God call his entire creation into being? Scripture declares, 'For God so loved the *world*' (John 3:16, literally "cosmos" or "universe"); how does his love *for me* fit inside his love for *the entire universe*?"

Using a zoom lens this way helps us to picture four concentric circles. The outermost circle represents God's calling the entire universe into existence, and the next "layer" points to God calling his people to shine like a light in his world. The third circle might be labeled "God's call to me to live as his

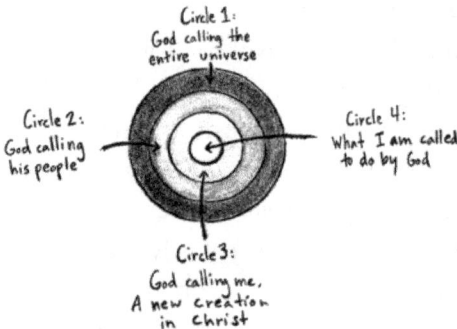

Circle 1:
God calling the entire universe

Circle 2:
God calling his people

Circle 4:
What I am called to do by God

Circle 3:
God calling me,
A new creation in Christ

child," which is the call to be a new creation in Christ, to die to the old person and to put on the new. It's not until we arrive at the innermost circle that we hear the question, "What am I called to do?" Moving step by step from the biggest possible picture to the most narrowly focused one puts a firmer foundation under that final question.

The Big Picture:
The Faithful God Calls His Entire Creation

Occasionally I have a conversation with a student who has not been very consistent in completing his assignments. After I have encouraged the struggling student to improve his performance, he often says something like, "I'll turn it around. You can count on me. I give you my word." At that point, I usually find myself looking deeply into the student's eyes, silently asking myself, "Does he really mean this or is he trying to get out of my office as quickly as possible? Will his actions back up his words?"

Part of being human is that there's always a gap between what we say and what we do. One of the deepest truths about God is that his actions and his words always match up completely. Not only does God make promises that he keeps, but he also speaks to his creation in such a way that *it is what he says*. *Calling* is a *speech* term. As the Lord declares, "Let there be light!" in Genesis 1:3, followed by all of the other "let there bes" of the creation, we see that everything that exists exists because God has called it into being. God calls, creation responds; that's where calling begins.

Circle 1:
God calling the entire universe

In other words, the search to understand what God calls me to do begins by remembering that *every molecule that exists* was called by God. That children's song has it right: "He's got the whole world in his hands." My life fits inside a picture that is much greater than just me. Remember Job? He endured extreme hardships in his life: his children and most of his servants were killed, he lost his possessions, he became very sick, and his wife finally advised him to "curse God and die" (Job 2:9). These hardships led him to question whether God was fair, or, in other words, whether life in God's world still made sense. Does God really hold the whole world in his hands? When the Lord comes to speak with Job in four very remarkable chapters (Job 38–41), the Lord does not speak about Job's suffering or whether God is fair. Rather, the Lord talks about his relationship with the entire universe. Listen to a brief excerpt:

> Who laid [the earth's] cornerstone while the morning stars sang together and all the angels shouted for joy? Who shut up the sea behind doors when it burst forth from the womb, when I made the clouds its garment and wrapped it in thick darkness, when I fixed limits for it and set its doors and bars in place, when I said, "This far you may come and no farther; here is where your proud waves halt"? Have you ever given orders to the morning, or shown the dawn its place? (Job 38:6b–12)

It's as though the Lord is saying to Job, "don't just fixate on your relationship with me. You are one creature inside the entire creation that I am taking care of; keep the big picture in mind." We read similar words during a time of national suffering, when Judah is in exile. The Israelites are wondering whether they will ever exist as a nation, as God's chosen people, again. The Lord responds forcefully:

> This is what the Lord says, he who appoints the sun to shine by day, who decrees the moon and stars to shine by night, who stirs up the sea so that its waves roar—the Lord Almighty is his name: "Only if these decrees vanish from my sight," declares the Lord "will the descendants of Israel ever cease to be a nation before me." (Jeremiah 31:35–36)

The bottom line is this: God calls the entire universe into being and holds it in place. He gave his word, and everything that exists can count on it. "Great is thy faithfulness" is one of the most beloved Christian hymns of all time, partly because it expresses this aspect of God's character so well.

What difference does it make that God's call to me comes inside his call to the entire universe? It feels like one of those "nice spiritual things to say" that doesn't really mean very much. Maybe it helped Job after his life fell apart, but most of the time my life is quite ordinary, thank you, and I'm just trying to figure out what job will make me happy and pay the mortgage.

Some years ago, I was flying into Vancouver, British Columbia, and had endured a turbulent flight through storm clouds over the Rocky Mountains. As we neared the coast, the sky cleared and there before us lay the deep blue of the Pacific, dotted with dark green islands and bordered by snow-capped mountains that crowded right up to the shore. That memory helps me understand calling. Storm clouds easily limit my vision; all I can see is my own turbulent situation and its confusions. But when the clouds clear, I stand in awe at the Creator of all nations and peoples, remembering that every Sunday he is worshiped through thousands of different languages in hundreds of different settings, ranging from the gathering in the outdoor jungle clearing to the dark and secretive Chinese cellar to the corner church on Main Street, USA. The Lord's call to me is one melody in a majestic chorus that includes billions of stars, sea creatures great and small, the wisdom of cultures ancient and contemporary all over the globe.

Because God's call to me comes inside his calling of the entire universe, when I pray, "Lord, help me to hear your call to me," I am actually praying, "your kingdom come, your will be done on earth as it is in heaven." This world belongs to God, and everything that I am called to be and do fits inside that prayer, "Our Father in heaven, hallowed be your name." The Holy One speaks, and his voice evokes an echo of holiness from his world. As one contemporary hymn puts it,

Holy is the setting of each room and yard
Lecture hall and kitchen, office, shop and ward.
Holy is the rhythm of our working hours;
Hallow then our purpose, energy and powers.

("Father, Help Your People," v. 3)

Everything that I do becomes part of a sacrifice of praise, a life of worship to God. God is hallowed through the careful repairing of cars, the thankful eating of nourishing meals, conversations through which we build each other up, the discerning reading of good books.

But there's another side to hearing God's call to us inside his call to his world: the response of the universe to God's call is always filled with agony because it cannot match the holiness of the one who calls. Paul tells us that "the whole creation has been groaning as in the pains of childbirth right up to the present time" (Romans 8:22). Part of our calling in the innermost circle is to listen carefully to the groaning of God's world. Paul also tells us that this groaning creation "waits in eager expectation for the sons of God to be revealed" (Romans 8:19). All of us—male and female—are the sons of God that the creation is crying out to. Imagine a tree groaning as you walk by, "I can't wait to see what God has called you to be and do so that you can help me to be what God has called me to be." God's personal call to each of us happens inside both the praising and the groaning of his creation. Probably the most famous statement about calling in Christian literature comes from Frederick Buechner, who writes, "the place God calls you is the place where your deep gladness and the world's deep hunger meet."* This outermost circle of calling challenges us to listen to and care about the world's deep hunger.

---

* *Wishful Thinking: A Theological ABC* (New York: Harper and Row, 1973), 95.

One of the goals of the Christian life is to hear the world's deep hunger more clearly. Frequently this hearing involves a greater awareness of the suffering present in our world and ways in which we can respond to that suffering. As this awareness grows, we also grow in seeing how easy it is to become oblivious and callous to the world's hunger. One college graduate I know found a well-paying job installing $100,000 entertainment centers in the homes of the extremely wealthy. After some time, he couldn't do it anymore—his fifty-hour weeks seemed to be entirely in the service of false hungers of the affluent that only mocked the world's truly deep hungers. His job change is part of a large trend in which more and more people are going through significant career changes at some point in their lives. One of the strongest factors influencing many Christians to change career paths comes directly from Romans 8: hearing the world's deep hunger and groaning more clearly leads to a shift in one's priorities and therefore to a shift in career as well.

In summary, as we fix our eyes on the universe the Lord has called into being, we see four different pictures. We see a *playground,* a wonderful garden of delights in which rabbits chase each other across flowered meadows and stars appear to dance on cloudless nights. We see a *workshop* in which there are thousands of different tasks for us to do. We see a *battleground,* a field filled with intense struggle between the power of God and forces that are determined to undermine his goodness. And finally, we see an *intensive care unit,* a place filled with the groans of creatures longing for all things to be made new.

As a child, Theresa always loved nature as God's *playground;* she developed this love as she became a research biologist. She was hired by a pharmaceutical company, and it sent her to the Arizona desert, which became her *workshop* for analyzing the healing qualities of a rare plant that grows there. Soon she found herself on a *battleground:* an environmental lobby group protested her work, arguing that this plant was so rare and the habitat so fragile that scientific intervention would endanger this plant species. This lobbying convinced Theresa that her desert playground/workshop was also an *intensive care unit*.

My wife and I have been married for almost thirty years, thankful that God's playground includes the blessing of committed love but very aware that such love requires a neverending workshop of faithfulness. North American culture is an antimarriage battleground, and it's easy for marriages to spend time in the intensive care unit on life support systems. God's call to us comes in many different areas of our lives; as we hear those calls inside his call to the entire universe, that odd mixture of playground/workshop/battleground/intensive care unit puts his call into a deeper perspective.

God Calls a Community into Being

This "creation calling" in the first, outer circle sets the stage for narrowing the picture to see a second circle of calling: God calls his people to be a *community* that reflects his light in the world. Peter's memorable words describe this call well:

Circle 2: God calling his people

> You are a chosen people, a royal priesthood, a holy nation, a people belonging to God, that you may declare the praises of him who called you out of darkness into his wonderful light. (1 Peter 2:9)

Just as the call to the universe began with the creation of light, so the call to God's people is a call to come *into* God's wonderful light to *reflect* that light. As God's people respond to that call, they "shine like stars in the universe as [they] hold out the word of life" (Philippians 2:15–16). Jesus is the Light of the world; we the Christian community are lampstands that hold up that Light (John 1:9, Revelation 1:20).

When I was a child in Sunday school, we sang, "Jesus bids us shine with a pure, clear light, like a little candle burning in the night . . . you in your small corner, and I in mine." As I sang, I pictured millions of tiny candles aflame in millions of dark corners; as an adult, I realized that this is quite different from the picture we find in Scripture. Scripture consistently speaks of a *communal* light, of the people of God *together* shining in Jesus, not in millions of isolated corners. On the Pentecost birthday of the church, three thousand people were added to the community (Acts 2:41), and the description of this amazing birth does not focus on individual lives that were changed, but on what the community did together: praying, learning, eating, taking care of the poor, having fellowship (Acts 2:42–47). Their life together was shaped by the Holy Spirit, and inside that communal shaping, individual lives were transformed.

Ponder for a moment all of the people who have contributed to forming you—family, friends, teachers, pastors, other church leaders, employers, authors, and musicians—as well as the events that have connected you to others. God's call to you and me has come inside a community. I carry inside myself a "community of the heart" and find there the gentle Christian farmer I worked for during my high school summers (who died twenty years ago), a Bible study group my wife and I belonged to during our thirties, thousands of worship services shared with communities that nourished us, conversations too numerous to count.

The second circle involves God calling his people to be a light in his world. This circle clearly flows from the previous one. Just as light shines in darkness, so God calls his people to address the world's greatest joys and hungers. God's call to his entire people reminds me that I do not search alone. Because I am part of the body of Christ, a worldwide community, many others encourage and advise me as I seek to discern my calling. I see role models all around me, and they spark my imagination with thoughts such as, "that fits with who I am." As I come to know the Christian community, I recognize that there are certain areas where there are simply not enough Christians involved, whereas there are other areas where there may even be too many at work. I recognize that there's more "deep hunger" in those places where too few are engaged.

Churches, Christian colleges, and other Christian organizations might be called "second circle institutions," places that link the outer circle of God's call to his creation with the inner circle of God's call to each of us. For example, Christian colleges (or Christian ministries on secular campuses) were formed by communities of Christians to help young men and women hear the voice of both their own deep gladness and the world's deep hunger. Christians who were raised in relatively affluent middle-class communities frequently come to hear the world's deep hunger in new ways when they grow into deeper understandings of poverty, family dysfunction, and racial injustice. When one comes to hear this hunger in new ways, that hearing may lead to choosing a new major or it may lead to recognizing in a new way the possibilities of one's already chosen major. As this hearing happens, the outer two circles of the "calling process" shape one's struggles with the question "what am I called to do?" in the innermost circle.

I Am Called to Be a New Creation in Christ

Next, the narrowing of God's call to us focuses on the question, "Who has God called me to be?" I am called to become a *certain kind of person;* the Holy Spirit transforms *my identity.* The Bible provides dozens of words and phrases that describe the new person that we are on the way to becoming in Christ. Such a person is characterized by love, joy, peace, patience, kindness, goodness, gentleness, faithfulness, self-control (Galatians 5:22–23), compassion, humility, a forgiving spirit, gratitude (Colossians 3:12–15), faith, love, endurance, hope (1 Thessalonians 1:3), and much more. In a certain sense, before I am called to *do* certain things, I am called to *be* God's child. A prayer composed centuries ago and still commonly used in Christian worship reflects this emphasis. Listen to it carefully:

Circle 3: God calling me: A new creation in Christ.

> Merciful God, we confess that we have sinned against you in thought, word, and deed, by what we have done and by what we have left undone. We have not loved you with our whole heart and mind and strength. We have not loved our neighbors as ourselves. In your mercy, forgive what we have been, help us amend what we are, and direct what we shall be, so that we may delight in your will and walk in your ways, to the glory of your holy name. Amen.

Listen to those words again: "forgive what we have been, help us amend what we are, and direct what we shall be." Why is it important to be a certain kind of person? Part of the answer lies in the outer two circles. It takes a certain kind of person to be able to listen to the groaning of God's good but broken world, just as it takes a certain kind of person to find her place inside the people of God. If I am not patient, self-controlled, hopeful, and humble, I will find it almost impossible to listen to the creation's groaning. I will tend to think to myself, "the world is too big and too troubled for me to worry about. Let me just find my own way and do what works out for me. I don't need the big picture; I just need what I can see right in front of my eyes." Similarly, if I am not a person of peace, gentleness, and endurance with a forgiving spirit, I will not be inclined to find my place within the Christian community. Instead, I'll tend to say things like, "Many Christians I know are judgmental and self-centered; worshiping with them tends to be boring and ir-relevant, and they don't seem to pay much attention to the groaning of the world—so why should I?"

Both of these thoughts have something true about them. Yes, the world is too big and troubled for me to fix. Yes, all Christians that I know are sinners. But these "truths" are placed inside God's call—his call to his creation, to his community, and to me—and inside that call, I say, "but he is God and he calls me to partner with his love for his groaning creation," and "but he is God, and he is making his people new just as he is making me new."

In some ways, "who am I called to be?" is a dangerous ques-tion. We may conclude that we must fit into some kind of "cookie cutter" mold, some kind of "good Christian clone," try-ing to be a certain way because that's the way Jesus wants us to be. I have met dozens of lovely Christian believers who consid-ered themselves "spiritually inferior" because they didn't fit the "holiness standards" of their Christian communities. What a horrible heresy! If we pull up a few biblical characters on our mental computer screens, we will notice how wonderfully di-verse they are. The ragtag group that surrounded Jesus during his ministry did not grow into faceless Jesus clones. As we ma-ture into our calling to become a new creation in Christ, we be-come more truly ourselves, able to celebrate and enjoy our differences and our diversity. In 1 Corinthians 12, Paul tells us that the body of Christ is one body with many different parts, and one of the chief challenges of this body is to recognize all of its many diverse parts and to honor the unique place that each one has.

We live in a culture where too often we are defined by what we do rather than by whom God is making us to be. When we meet someone new, one of the earliest questions in the conver-sation is, "so, what do you do?" and the answer we receive often goes into the mix by which we assess what this person is like. Our culture's salary structures reinforce this evaluation: one person's worth is measured at minimum wage and another's at millions of dollars per year. God, however, does not assess our worth by what we do. He makes us *new people* in Christ. "For it is by grace you have been saved, through faith—and this not from yourselves, it is the gift of God—not by works, so that no one can boast" (Ephesians 2:8–9). In this third circle, I am set free from the burden of having to *prove* that I am a worthwhile person because of what I do or plan to do.

A few years ago, I read a magazine article about the "imposter syndrome." This condition is one in which a person is considered a success by everyone: by employers, teachers, peers, and so on. The person is aware that she is considered a success, but deep down, she thinks, "I guess I've just faked them all out. If they really knew how incompetent I was most of the time, none of them would consider me to be successful." The article struck me because it described exactly how I felt about my job at the time. Since then, I've learned that many people struggle with the imposter syndrome, and it has its roots in finding our identity in what we do instead of who we are in Christ.

To understand calling as four circles also sets us free from the burden of feeling compelled to choose exactly the right thing to do. Calling is so much bigger than that one question! The first three circles provide a great deal of guidance and a great deal of freedom concerning the question in the innermost circle, "what am I called to do?"

Chapter Three

Our Identity

Inside God's Calling

It's not just the culture that tends to define my identity in terms of what I do. It's easy to treat the Bible as a book that focuses on this as well. A few years ago, millions of Christians wore armbands inscribed with WWJD—"What would Jesus do?"—as a way of reminding themselves to act in ways appropriate to Jesus. Those armbands undoubtedly served a good purpose, but they also reinforced a way of reading the Bible that limits its power. The Bible is not first of all concerned with what we do; it is first concerned with who God is and what God does, then flows from there to describing who God is making us (and his world) to be. When we read it as a book telling us what to do, we read it as a rulebook, and it becomes very easy for the Christian life to be reduced to simple legalism. Much of the Bible seems fairly pointless if our purpose is to find simple rules for living. Condensing the Bible into a rulebook could probably be done in about fifty pages; why do we need to read almost twelve hundred chapters instead?

John Calvin, one of the wise leaders of the Protestant Reformation, provides helpful advice. In his *Institutes of the Christian Religion* (§37) we read,

> Nearly all the wisdom we possess, that is to say, true and sound wisdom, consists of two parts: the knowledge of God and of ourselves.

In this sentence, Calvin lays one part of the foundation of our connection to the story of the Bible. The Bible tells the story of

God's faithfulness to his creation, and as we come to know the story, we come to know God. But that story is *our* story, too; as we come to know the story, we come to know ourselves more clearly. Knowledge of God and knowledge of ourselves are completely intertwined. Growing in understanding concerning the identity of God and our own identity lies at the center of our reading of Scripture.

Our identity flows from God's identity. As we grow in knowing him, we recognize that the Bible invariably talks about him in relational terms: the Father of his children, the husband of his bride, the shepherd of his sheep, and so on. When we who are the children, the bride, and the sheep describe ourselves, we eventually recognize that knowing ourselves requires seeing how we have been shaped by the Father, the husband, the shepherd. Our lives are lived inside the story of God. This truth makes reading the Bible unique! Usually when I read something, I take it in and it finds its place inside me. But when I read the Bible, it *takes me in* so that I find my place inside it.

Hans-Ruedi Weber tells this story from East Africa that helps us to understand how this process works.

> A simple woman always walked around with a bulky Bible. Never would she part from it. Soon the villagers began to tease her. "Why always the Bible? There are so many books you could read!" Yet the woman kept on living with her Bible, neither disturbed nor angered by all the teasing. Finally, one day she knelt down in the midst of those who laughed at her. Holding the Bible high above her head, she said with a big smile, "Yes, of course there are many books which I could read. But there is only one book which reads me!"[†]

---

† Quoted by Craig Dykstra in *Growing in the Life of Faith* (Louisville: Geneva Press, 1999), 52.

She wonderfully describes both the joy and the challenge of life inside the story of God: the book reads us because God knows us inside out and shapes who we are.

The Image of God:
Personal Wiring and Worship that Reflects

The biblical phrase that helps us unpack the connection between knowledge of God and our knowledge of ourselves—what Calvin calls "true and sound wisdom"—is "image of God." Who are we? We have been created in the image of God. What does that mean? It requires understanding as much as we can concerning the character and actions of God. In a later chapter, we'll explore that phrase in some detail, but for now we'll look at one of its foundational characteristics: because we are made in God's image, (1) *we each have a unique personality*, and (2) *we reflect what we worship and trust*.

God is a *personal* God; he knows each one of us intimately (Psalm 139) and desires to be known by us intimately as well. Think of a person who both knows you well and cares for you deeply. That combination of being known and being loved is a *freeing* combination—it frees us up to be ourselves. The more intimate a relationship, the more fully our *real* self is invited to be engaged. When I pay my taxes, I am known primarily through my Social Security number; all that matters is that my check doesn't bounce. My personality, beliefs, relationships, and pasta preferences are all irrelevant. My wife, on the other hand, doesn't really care what my Social Security number is, but she frees me up to be myself with her. Similarly, the Christian faith worships a God who frees us up in ways that celebrate our uniquenesses.

Because God is a personal God, the Bible is filled with portraits of colorful persons. We meet hundreds of characters in the Bible, and who they are as people matters because that's the kind of God we have. We meet the prostitute Rahab who saves the lives of Jewish spies; Ruth the Moabitess who stubbornly refuses to let her mother-in-law return to Israel alone; Isaiah the passionate young prophet who boldly declares, "Here I am, send me!"; Zaccheus the short tax collector who was eager to see Jesus walking by; Peter the impulsive disciple whose words were either right on or way off. The Christian faith is not about faceless, clothed-in-gray comrades, but brothers and sisters in the Lord loved into a wholeness that allows us to be more fully ourselves. We are blessed with God-given wiring—a unique way of being put together.

Our uniqueness can be developed to serve the Lord or to serve other interests. Think of the apostle Paul. Before he became a Christian, he was a driven, ambitious leader determined to persecute Christians wherever they could be found. After Jesus turned his life around, he was still a driven, ambitious, and determined leader, but now his wiring was transformed and placed at the service of the coming of God's kingdom. The wiring that God created him with did not change, but the orientation of this wiring did change.

And that brings us to the second part: because we are created in the image of God, we reflect what we worship and trust. Worship comes from the old English word *worthship*. Something in our lives takes on ultimate *worth,* and therefore we "worthship" it. Our worship indicates that we place trust in this reality of ultimate worth. As we trust and worship this reality, we begin to reflect it, we become more like it.

Our reflection of what we worship and trust points on the one hand to profound beauty and wonder. The sovereign God of the entire universe allows us to reflect him in certain ways as we worship and trust him! That's too grand for me to comprehend. Bits of his grace, love, joy, patience, kindness, and so on shine through us in the same way that the moon reflects the light of the sun. During a time of difficult struggle against his "thorn in the flesh," the apostle Paul heard the Lord say to him, "my grace is sufficient for you, for my power is made perfect in weakness" (2 Corinthians 12:9). It's as though God said to his confused servant, "simply rest in my grace and you will reflect me; you will be my image, the image of God." I find that to be one of the most comforting declarations in the entire Bible.

But there's also something terrifying about being made to reflect what we worship and trust. What happens when I worship and trust false gods? Will I reflect them instead and become like them? Listen to Psalm 115: "Those who make idols will be like them, and so will all who trust in them" (v. 8). This means that to be created in the image of God is to be created *moldable,* that is, our identity—who we are—changes according to what lies at the center of our lives, what owns our hearts. Jesus puts it this way: "Do not store up for yourselves treasures on earth, where moth and rust destroy and thieves break in and steal. But store up for yourselves treasures in heaven, where moth and rust do not destroy, and where thieves do not break in and steal. For where your treasure is, there your heart will be also" (Matthew 6:19–21). And where our heart goes, our identity follows, or, to use the words of Augustine, "Each is such as is his love." Put even more simply, "We become what we love").

When I ask Christians to name the most common false gods that tempt us, money and material possessions always top the list. Do we become like money if we trust in it? There's a common saying in our culture that refers to money as "cold, hard cash." We can picture someone saying, "I've had enough of your empty promises; just show me the cold, hard cash." Could that simple phrase have a deeper spiritual meaning? People that I know who have allowed money and material possessions to become the central driving force in their lives appear—after many years of such pursuit—to become cold, hard people. When money takes precedence over my friendships, my marriage and family, my faith in God—in other words, everything—then all of those other aspects of my life will develop a type of cold hardness about them. It's no wonder that in a culture where money is so important, so many marriages fail and so many children sense that their parents are willing to give them everything they want except real love.

The Serpent's Distortion of the Image of God

This "wonderful yet terrifying" character of our creation in the image of God is revealed with poignant clarity in Genesis 3. After God's good creation was completed, the serpent studied God's masterpiece and recognized its place of vulnerability: humankind created in the image of God. Because Adam and Eve were created to reflect God as they trusted and worshiped him, the serpent recognized that they would also reflect other realities if they trusted and worshiped something else instead. Traditionally we read Genesis 3 as a description of humankind *doing* the wrong thing: eating the forbidden fruit. That traditional understanding is partly correct: they do the wrong thing because they succumb to a temptation to change their *identity,* to become something they are not. The sin of *what they do* is rooted in the sin of who they desire *to be.*

The drama begins when the serpent says to the woman (Eve), "Did God really say that you must not eat from any of the trees in the garden?" and she assures him that actually there is only one tree that they may not touch, or they will die. "You will not surely die," he replies, "for God knows that when you eat of it, your eyes will be opened, and you will be like God, knowing good and evil" (Genesis 3:4–5). One simple sentence, and yet this one sentence is one of the most clever sentences in the entire Scripture.

Let's look at it closely. The sentence refers to three parties that are all interrelated: the tree, God, and humankind. In Genesis 2, these three fit together inside a wondrous whole of shalom. God lovingly forms a man from the clay of the earth and blows the breath of life into him. God plants trees in that same clay; both humankind and the trees trace their "roots" back to the clay. He gives man and woman the instruction to tend the trees in the garden, and this tending is how man and woman reflect God's image on the earth. There is one tree that they will tend by leaving it completely alone; only God will tend this one particular tree, so that this one tree declares that there is a boundary between humankind and God. Shalom is shaped by an intimate union between God, his creation, and his human creatures, but shalom also requires a boundary between humankind and God (after all, he is the infinite Creator and they are his creatures). The picture is one of overflowing grace; there is gift and blessing and fruitfulness everywhere. Inside this picture, man and woman find their identity: created from elements of the creation, made in the image of God, given a task to do together, they are creatures blessed by gift and responsibility.

The serpent knows that disturbing this picture of deep shalom will require attacking the whole picture, the picture that includes God, humankind, and creation. He twists that picture horribly. In one sentence, the entire triangle of shalom is distorted: the tree that points to a boundary of blessing becomes a tree of terrible secrets. God is no longer the giver and lover and provider; God becomes the keeper of secrets. God knows that when you eat of this tree you will be like him. God is the nervously insecure tyrant, desperately hoping that his secret for holding on to power will not be found so that he can keep humankind in its inferior position. And, finally, the identity of humankind becomes twisted as well: to be human is to be kept deliberately inferior, deprived of something the serpent considers to be essential, the ability to be like God. Therefore, human identity no longer reflects the loving, gracious, wondrous Creator God. Instead, human identity reflects a false god created by the serpent; human identity reflects a nervous, secretive, power-hungry god. No longer do shalom and trust live in the center of human identity; rather, it is shaped by anxiety and fear and power struggle. We were created to live at rest in the heart of God; due to the serpent's distortion, we are grasping in competition with God instead. It's no surprise that immediately after the fall into sin, both Adam and Eve become nervous and secretive, hiding from God and from each other (Genesis 3:7–8). They have become like that which they have worshiped, a false god, an idol created by the serpent.

Living Radio Receivers

That struggle between true worship of God and false worship of idols is part of every Christian believer's life. Imagine that each one of us is like a living radio receiver. The atmosphere around us is filled with the airwaves from hundreds of radio stations. One station broadcasts the truth, all of the others broadcast lies. Every receiver is capable of tuning in many stations; some come in loud and clear, others are faint and filled with static. The fundamental message of the one true station proclaims, "Nothing can separate us from the love of God in Jesus Christ our Lord" (Romans 8:39). Other stations have identifying call names such as "You are what you look like," "You are what you accomplish," "You are what you own," "Life sucks, and you're all alone," and many more such "you are" state-

ments. Most of us live with our radios tuned to two or three stations at the same time, and through a confusing jumble, we try to discern God's truth.

This might work out in daily life like this: Becky, who studies at a Christian college in Iowa, hails from Minnesota, has light brown hair, loves basketball, has to work hard for her grades, dreams of becoming a physiotherapist, worships at an Evangelical Free church, is the youngest of four children, has some trouble sleeping because of anxiety, sings alto in the choir, and hates pasta. These ten facts sound just like most of our lives: wonderfully ordinary. When we tune these details of Becky's life into the radio station that declares, "nothing can separate Becky from the love of God," those facts may stay the same but *the way they fit together* is affected. She experiences regular times of anxiety, and she frequently reminds herself, "Hang in there, Beck, God has seen you through hard times in the past and he won't quit on you now." Some days when she says this, she doesn't totally believe it but she says it anyway because part of her knows that the reality of God is stronger than her feelings and doubts. She finds that the three choir practices she attends each week are like devotional times for her; many of the choral pieces speak directly to her heart and strengthen the words on Radio Station One. She knows that as an E-Free member she's part of a minority at her Reformed college, but she's also noticed that many others quietly respect her background and enjoy speaking with her because conversations between students of differing church backgrounds tend to clarify everyone's convictions. The deepest truth about ourselves— the truth of who we are in Christ—has a shaping power over all of the "facts" of our lives.

The deepest truth about Becky's life is that she is loved by God, but on her bad days another radio station takes over, one that broadcasts, "Life sucks and you're all alone." Notice how some of the ten facts look differently through each of these two messages. This radio station says to Becky, "You'd better be anxious because good grades don't come easily for you, and your E-Free connection means you'll always feel somewhat out of place at a Reformed, Christian college." There are two roommates on her wing from a local Reformed church, and whenever Becky passes them in the hall (it seems like they're always together), the look in their eyes tells Becky that she's inferior because her denomination just doesn't measure up. That feeling of being put down interferes with her studying, weakening some of her drive and determination. She thinks, "Grades come hard for me and college is supposed to be fun. Who cares about physiotherapy? I'll try harder next semester." The details of her life look and feel different when they are lived through that other radio station.

And that's how God created us: who we are changes—sometimes dramatically—according to who or what it is that we allow to define who we are. God in his grace has declared the truth, which shapes us before him, but those other messages do not let go easily and continue to compete for the primary place.

This identity competition takes place inside the human heart. The Bible describes our heart as the center of our being, that part of us that holds us together as more-or-less unified beings. A passage that many believers know by memory goes like this: "Trust in the Lord with all your heart, and lean not on your own understanding; in all your ways acknowledge him, and he will make your paths straight" (Proverbs 3:5–6). The heart is the *organ of trust,* which means that it is incomplete on its own. It is created to look for that which is trustworthy and to orient itself to the trustworthy one. That's why Augustine writes, "Our hearts are restless, Lord, until they find their rest in you." Trust is the central dimension of faith. At times, believers reduce faith to acknowledging that God exists; in response to this limited view of faith, James replies, "You believe that there is one God. Good! Even the demons believe that—and shudder" (James 2:19). Acknowledgment is not faith unless it is partnered with a trusting surrender that engages the heart as it was meant to do.

When we allow the Bible to read us by living our lives inside the story of God, we recognize that we have divided hearts, giving part of our heart to the Lord and the rest to other competitors. Abraham trusted in the Lord as he left his homeland, but shortly thereafter trusted in his own understanding by persuading his wife Sarah to deceive Pharaoh (Genesis 12:1–20); David trusted in the Lord when he faced Goliath, but in later years, David trusted in the strength of his armies (1 Chronicles 21:1–30); the Bible warns against trusting in wealth, in powerful friends, in future plans, in idols of wood or stone. We don't bow down to idols of wood or stone today because the primary competitors for our trust are generally provided by the culture in which we live, and those older sorts of idols simply aren't part of our present cultural context. Instead, we are tempted to bow down to wealth, financial security, our appearance, our achievements, and even our theology or the doctrines of our denomination. Trusting in the Lord with all of our heart involves putting to death our temptations to trust in God's competitors and growing in trust of the Lord alone, allowing him to be the primary one who shapes our identity.

Identity Inside the Family

Have you ever tried explaining the doctrine of the Trinity to someone unfamiliar with the Christian faith? It's a challenge: "Well, there's one God, but he comes in three persons; each one is different, though they're the same God. . . ." I once heard a preacher describe the Trinity as a family: "There is God the Father, and his Son Jesus Christ, and they share an intense love beyond description. Their love for each other is strengthened by the Holy Spirit, and they pour out the Spirit so that many others might become part of the family, too." John's gospel supports this description: "In the beginning was the Word [Jesus], and the Word was with God, and the Word was God. . . . To all who received him, to those who believed in his name, he gave the right to become children of God" (John 1:1, 12). God is a family overflowing with love, eager to bring many more into the family of God.

Many years ago, my wife and I attended a workshop for parents who had adopted children. The leader, who also was an adoptive parent, gave this analogy: "A family," he said, "is like the frame of a house in which many different pieces of lumber are solidly nailed together. In an adoptive family, it's like there are fewer nails holding the wood together, and so the parents have to work harder to maintain a strong framework for the home."

The Bible says that Christians are adopted children of God (Ephesians 1:5), and that same principle holds true in the family of God. The Bible is filled with images and metaphors that describe our connectedness to God and his people. Jesus is the vine and we are the branches (John 15); he is the head and we are the body (Ephesians 4); he is the cornerstone and we are living stones (Ephesians 2, 1 Peter 2); we are clothed with Christ (Galatians 3, Colossians 3, Romans 13); Jesus is the foundation and we are the building (1 Corinthians 3). All of these images and metaphors are designed to add more nails to the frame that builds the family of God, to strengthen the process of adopting us into the family.

The "who am I called to be" question is both a personal question and a family question. I am called to be a child of the Father, redeemed by the Son, growing in the Spirit to become more fully the child he has made me to be. The story of God is the story that covers the entire universe from the very first "Let there be . . ." and on into eternity, into the new creation. In comparison, the story of my life is like a drop in the ocean, and yet God tells me that the story of my life matters intensely inside the story of God, and it is fully connected there as well. The Christian faith has come to use three theological terms as a kind of "family vocabulary" to help us to see how this intense connectedness works: *justification, sanctification,* and *glorification.* These three terms point to the *origin and foundation* of our connectedness, the *maturing* of our connectedness, and its *completion* or *consummation.* These three terms describe how God transforms our identity.

Justification

Justification is a term that has its roots in the court systems: I am declared innocent in the name of Jesus Christ; the blood of the Lamb covers me. As the judge delivers the "not guilty" verdict, it's as though he places a new identity in my hand as a free gift that declares "I am loved by God" and tunes me in to the radio station that broadcasts this profound truth. With this new identity, I am adopted into the family of God and receive the gift of the Holy Spirit. Many children are taught to define the result of justification as "just as if I had never sinned," and that phrase captures the reality well. It is a gift of grace (which other children have learned with the acronym "God's Riches At Christ's Expense"). Paul's summary of this truth is a favorite of many believers: "It is by grace you have been saved, through faith—and this not from yourselves, it is the gift of God—not by works, so that no one can boast" (Ephesians 2:8–9).

A gift is given in the context of a relationship, and receiving the gift of justification involves more than meets the eye. Receiving justification sounds terribly easy, but in reality, it is a powerfully difficult challenge. To be justified is to be *born again,* and to be born again means that I must die to be brought to new life. Paul writes, "I have been crucified with Christ, and I no longer live, but Christ lives in me" (Galatians 2:20a). Sometimes Christians describe justification as the forgiveness of our sins, as though we are carrying a huge, heavy bag on our backs that burdens us with all of our sins, and through Jesus's death on the cross, the bag is removed and we can walk without stooping, set free. There is some truth to that analogy, but it doesn't go deep enough. It's not just that our sins are removed; we are put to death! Our old self is removed. The false radio stations that oriented and guided our lives are dethroned and a new radio station is tuned in to take its place. The sound of that new radio station covers our entire being; believers acknowledge this effect by declaring at times, "I am covered by the blood of the Lamb." Covered by the blood, we stand on a new foundation upon which we grow into new persons. Justified believers are given a new identity to grow toward. Because I have been justified, my life has value and purpose.

Sanctification

The work of justification is complete, finished, accomplished, but God's work in our lives is not done. Life with God is shaped by a delicious paradox: to be justified is to be born again, but as born again believers we die and rise to new life in Christ *every day.* Paul captures this paradox well in Colossians 3, where he writes, "For you died, and your life is now hidden with Christ in God. . . . Put to death, therefore, whatever belongs to your earthly nature . . ." (vv. 3, 5a). The believer has died and received the gift of new life (justification); the believer lives in a pattern of daily dying and rising (sanctification). This daily pattern is the shape of maturing in Christ, becoming more like him as our old self dies and the new self shaped by the Holy Spirit comes to life.

The New Testament contains many descriptions of God's work of justification and sanctification. One of the most beautiful is found in a hymn sung to Jesus in the book of Revelation:

> You [Jesus] are worthy to take the scroll
> and to open its seals,
> because you were slain, and with your blood
> you purchased men for God
> from every tribe and language and people and nation.
> You have made them to be a kingdom and priests to serve our God,
> and they will reign on the earth. (Revelation 5:9–10)

This hymn to Jesus describes his gifts of justification ("purchased men for God") and sanctification ("made them to be a kingdom and priests") to believers. Believers who are being sanctified participate in the coming of God's kingdom—seeking first that kingdom—as they die and rise with Jesus. They are priests (mediators between God and his creation) who bring the brokenness of the world to God and bring the blessings of God to the world.

There are crucial differences between justification and sanctification:

1. Justification is a gift; sanctification is both a gift and a responsibility.

When we are saved, we receive the Holy Spirit. Often the Holy Spirit is like a gentle guest within that says to us something like, "Thank you for allowing me to guide your dying and rising in Christ; I am here at your service." Because of his gentle manner, we can ignore and even suppress the Spirit's work in our lives (which is why Paul tells one church to take care that they "do not put out the Spirit's fire" [1 Thessalonians 5:19]). The Spirit invites us to get to work, to "work out our salvation with fear and trembling, for it is God who works in us to will and to act according to his good purpose" (Philippians 2:11–12). We do not work *for* our salvation; that is the gift of justification. Rather, we work *out* our salvation as God works *in us;* with the

Spirit, we build on the foundation established for us by the blood of the Lamb.

2. Justification is personal; sanctification is both personal and communal.

Jesus calls us each personally to come to the cross and be covered by his blood. As we live on that foundation, "it is not good for man to be alone" (Genesis 2:18). We need others to encourage us, challenge us, partner with us, pray for us and with us, worship with us, and on and on. To be a kingdom and priests is to be a community of Christ. As people joined to Christ, we are grafted into his body and we live for the sake of the world, to be a light and a salt. We are not only called to mature personally. We are called to be part of marriages, families, congregations, businesses, schools, social circles, service ministries, and citizenship groups. These communal entities are also called to mature. Through justification, the Lord says, "Your life story is now shaped by the story of my faithfulness." Through sanctification, the Lord continues, "And your story is intertwined with everyone else's stories as well."

3. Justification is complete; sanctification continues until we die or Jesus returns.

When Jesus cried out on the cross, "It is finished" (John 19:30), he declared that the work of redemption had been completed. The work of our justification is done; there's nothing more that must yet happen. But the *implications and consequences* of our justification are still being worked out through our sanctification. Toward the end of his life, Paul reflects on his own sanctification and concludes, "Not that I have already obtained all this [to be like Jesus], or have already been made perfect, but I press on to take hold of that for which Christ Jesus took hold of me" (Philippians 3:12). Sanctification is about pressing on, seeking to be faithful until we breathe our last on this earth. We can't postpone sanctification until we reach the "serious" years of middle age, and we never retire from it, either. If we are in Christ, he is working *in* us, *on* us, and *through* us from now into eternity.

4. Both justification and sanctification involve our entire being.

Jesus doesn't just save me from my sins; he saves me from my *self* and restores to me my *real* self, the one I am meant to be in Christ. "If anyone is in Christ, he is a new creation," declares Paul, "the old has gone, the new has come" (2 Corinthians 5:17). Salvation involves a refashioning of our identity, allowing ourselves to become more fully who we are meant to be. C. S. Lewis describes this process with a wonderful analogy:

> Imagine yourself as a living house. God comes in to rebuild that house. At first, perhaps, you can understand what he is doing. He is getting the drains right and stopping the leaks in the roof and so on: you knew that these jobs needed doing and so you are not surprised. But presently he starts knocking the house about in a way that hurts abominably and does not seem to make sense. What on earth is he up to? The explanation is that he is building quite a different house from the one you thought of . . . running up towers, making courtyards. You thought you were going to be made into a decent little cottage: but he is building a palace. He intends to come and live in it himself.
> (*Mere Christianity,* 160)

Glorification

Justification and sanctification are not the whole story. A foundation needs a *finished* house built on it; maturing grows toward a goal. We call the completion of these two gifts of God *glorification,* the making new of all things when Jesus returns and the new creation is ushered in. God is faithful, and he finishes what he begins, for "he who began a good work in you will carry it on to completion until the day of Christ Jesus" (Philippians 1:6).

Of these three works, the Bible has the least to say about glorification, perhaps because it is beyond our understanding. How can redeemed sinners imagine what perfect fullness and intimacy look like? John tells us that "now we are children of God, and what we will be has not yet been made known. But we know that when he appears we shall be like him, for we shall see him as he is" (1 John 3:2). What might it mean that "we shall be like Jesus?" I don't know—I only know that it will be marvelous beyond description. The Bible gives us other glimpses of glorification, too: "The wolf will live with the lamb, the leopard will lie down with the goat, the calf and the lion and the yearling together, and a little child will lead them. . . . They will neither harm nor destroy on all my holy mountain, for the earth will be full of the knowledge of the Lord as the waters cover the sea" (Isaiah 11:6, 9). "Then I saw a new heaven and a new earth, for the first heaven and the first earth had passed away. . . . There will be no more death or mourning or crying or pain, for the old order of things has passed away" (Revelation 21:1, 4). It's clear that the glorification of the entire creation involves an overflowing of *shalom*—everything right in every possible way.

God's work of redemption is like rippling circles in a pond that grow wider and wider and expand in the same way that the four circles of our zoom lens at the beginning of this chapter do. The first two ripples involve justification, which is personal and declares that God has transformed my identity.

Sanctification expands these circles to include the communal dimension of life, situating us inside the body of Christ, of which he is the head. God has called a community of many different members to be a salt and a light in the world, carrying out "works of service, so that the body of Christ may be built up until we all reach unity in the faith and in the knowledge of the Son of God and become mature, attaining to the whole measure of the fullness of Christ" (Ephesians 4:12–13).

Finally, glorification expands to the widest margins to include all of creation. Just as God called the entire universe into being through the "Let there bes" of Genesis 1, so he is calling a new creation into being that will be revealed when Jesus returns. The Christian life is a life founded on our justification, anticipating the glorification of all things, journeying along the way of sanctification. The Lord has said to us, "I have made you new; your life is not gray but it's shaped by living color. Walk with me everyday as together we deepen those colors, until we're ready for the entire creation to be bathed in the most intensely vibrant colors imaginable." Living between our foundation and our goal, sanctification describes every moment of our lives; that's *the central dimension* of our walk with Jesus. Therefore, the next two chapters will take a closer look at the dynamics of sanctification.

Chapter Four

Truth Walkers

I once heard a pastor say, "I visited a church member last night who has been a believer for forty years. But he's been a one-year-old Christian forty consecutive times."

This disappointed pastor was describing a Christian believer who refused to mature in his faith. This believer declared his belief in God, prayed for forgiveness every day, and lived his life in blissful ignorance of God's call to him to surrender every moment of his days and every molecule of his being to the God who claimed his life. Many times he had sung that great hymn of surrender, but its words on the page did not become a commitment on his heart:

> Take my life and let it be consecrated Lord to Thee.
> Take my moments and my days; let them flow in endless praise.
> Take my will and make it thine; it shall be no longer mine.
> Take my heart—it is thine own; it shall be thy royal throne.
> Take my love; my Lord, I pour at thy feet its treasure store.
> Take myself and I will be ever, only, all for Thee.

Frances Havergal's beautiful song is a prayerful commitment to surrender to God's maturing work. It's the song of a "truth walker," the kind of person the apostle John had in mind when he wrote, "I have no greater joy than to hear that my children are walking in the truth" (3 John 4). To walk in the truth is to embark upon the journey of growing in the truth, to allow the one who claims "I am the Way, the Truth and the Life" (John 14:6) to grow within us more and more fully.

What helps us to become truth walkers? What helps us to mature in our faith? Is it something *God* does (so all we can do is pray and hope that he will do it), or is there something *we* have to do, or is it a combination? How can we tell that maturation is occurring? What are the signs? Just as human life is a wondrous mystery beyond complete explanation, so God's work of transforming human life cannot be reduced to a recipe or formula.

I like to ask believers what is helping their growth toward Christian maturity. The five most common responses I have received over the years (in no particular order) are: (a) life difficulties, (b) role models, (c) special events, (d) good teaching, and (e) regular activities that strengthen faith life. This chapter focuses on the last one, but I will say just a bit about the others first.

Difficulties in life often function as faith wake-up calls: a grandparent dies, parents divorce, a high school friend dies in a car accident, a parent loses a job and the family's financial security is in jeopardy, an unplanned pregnancy occurs, a local church becomes hellish because of intense conflict, terrorists fly planes into high-rise buildings, an older sibling rejects God and breaks ties with the family. When life is "normal," we easily flow from day to day without asking the deeper "why" questions. But when tragedy or difficulty interrupts the normalcy, we are confronted with the big picture issues, such as, "Does God really hold the whole world in his hands?" "Is God as loving as everybody says?" "Why did this happen now to us?" Such questions can shift our believing from words that grip us only partially to an intense wrestling with God that reminds us of Jacob's wrestling with God.

Second, role models play a crucial role in the lives of truth walkers. Proverbs such as "don't just talk the talk but walk the walk" and "I don't care what you know until I know that you care" remind us that others influence us by their example and by their love. Some time ago, I attended the memorial service for a young man who graduated from college in May 2003. I was his adviser and taught him in several courses, and as I reflected on his short life, I realized that in several ways he had been a role model for me. He approached life with a carefree joy, a type of holy indifference concerning how others looked at him, and a down-to-earth faith. Many of the deepest aspects of truth walking are "caught, not taught," someone has said, and being with others who have captured bits of Spirit-led living allows that "contagious catching" to happen. Perhaps that's why so many verses in the Psalms and the Proverbs advise us to pay attention to the people we choose to surround ourselves with.

Third, many believers point to special events that have encouraged their faith life. These include mission trips, conventions, retreats, service projects, wilderness hikes, and more. A special event functions somewhat like a major life difficulty (though it's much more enjoyable) by interrupting the flow of regularity and thereby freeing one up to see the bigger picture and ponder deeper issues. In addition, a special event also interrupts the normal social patterns and introduces us to many new people who have also been freed up to ponder; this mutual freeing can create an environment of "quick intimacy" where someone who was almost a total stranger becomes a significant faith partner. Special events always carry the danger of manipulating participants into cheap spiritual highs that quickly wear off after the event ends, but just how potent this danger is depends on each participant's approach.

Fourth, growing toward Christian maturity requires solid teaching. This does not mean that we are to spend our entire lives in the classroom, because we are surrounded by teaching everywhere we go. Television and radio programs and videos teach us continually. Every life we connect with somehow has a teaching effect upon us. We are surrounded by a Babel of confusing teacher voices, and we need a core of solid, biblical teaching to keep us traveling in the right direction through that Babel. Teaching comes to us through worship and preaching, small group study, devotions, reading, conversations with wise people, discerningly observing what is going on in the world around us—as well as spending time in the classroom.

Imagine the overall picture of truth walking as a family dinner. We might say that special events are like the appetizer before the meal: delicious, whetting the appetite, but unsatisfying if not followed by more substantial fare. Difficulties can be like foods we would rather avoid, maybe Brussels sprouts or liver, that ultimately strengthen us but are not at all enjoyable. Role models are like our fellow diners; we learn from them which fork to use when, how to eat lobster, and how to display good table manners. Good teaching provides the ingredients for different recipes for preparing the food—hundreds of different recipes that cover every type of eating situation. One more dimension is needed: *regularity*. Maintaining well-nourished health requires eating nutritious food daily. This chapter will focus on the place of regularity—here called "truth-walking habits"—in the maturing of the believer.

Truth Walking as Prophetic Living

A little poem I loved as a child goes like this: "Don't worry if your job is small, and your rewards are few. Remember that the mighty oak was once a nut like you." That silly poem points to a central feature of "being sanctified": prophetic living. The poem tells us that where most people see nothing but a small nut lying on the ground, a person with vision sees the mighty oak inside the nut waiting to be planted so that it can grow. Such vision is *prophetic*. Prophetic vision has the gift to see beyond the surface of things to the deeper reality that lies hidden below. Prophetic vision is the gift of naming things for what they really are, which leads to prophetic living: walking in the *truth*.

Prophetic living is central to maturing in Christ because, in terms of the Biblical story, we live in the age of Pentecost, the time between Christ's ascension into heaven and his return from heaven. In Peter's sermon in Acts 2, the first thing that Scripture tells us about the age of Pentecost is that it is a time when God declares,

> I will pour out my Spirit on all people. Your sons and daughters will prophesy, your young men will see visions, your old men will dream dreams. Even on my servants, both men and women, I will pour out my spirit in those days, and they will prophesy. (vv. 17–18)

Life in the Spirit is shaped by a prophetic pattern, a pattern of declaring the truth in the name of the Lord, a pattern of naming things for what they truly are. If you are a Christian, you are a prophet: a truth speaker and a truth walker. Such speaking and walking begins with *seeing*: prophetic vision.

Psychologists tell us that our eyes are involved in two processes: sensation and perception. *Sensation* refers to our eyes' response to light and the resulting messages that are sent to the brain. Sensation is passive, taking in what the eyes "see." *Perception* has to do with making sense of the light messages that are sent to the brain; it is an active, constructive process. For example, my brain receives light messages of a large object that is swaying in the wind, with a thick, brown base and a wide crown filled with greenery and smaller brown lines. My brain then actively processes these sensations and decides that it has seen a tree. Such seeing is quite straightforward, but much of what we see in life is more complex; it requires decisions of perception that flow directly from our faith commitments and thus is called "prophetic vision."

For example, prophetic vision identifies sin even when it looks like peace, goodness, and well-being; it names the presence of God even when it looks like weakness and insignificance. We see prophetic vision in action when David is named as the new king of Israel even though he is the youngest and certainly not the most handsome of Jesse's many sons, for "man looks at the outward appearance, but the Lord looks at the heart" (1 Samuel 16:7). We see it when eleven confused and argumentative disciples are appointed as the apostles of the new church. We see it when a widow who drops two pennies into the collection plate is identified as more generous than the rich Pharisees who deposit their thousands (Luke 21:1–4). We see it when the rich church in Laodicea is named as poor while the poor church in Smyrna is named as rich (Revelation 3:17, 2:9). We see it when Paul dares to name suffering in terms of glory in both Romans 8 and 2 Corinthians 4.

Perhaps you are thinking to yourself, "what do these Bible passages have to do with being prophetic? They say nothing about future events." If so, you're in good company. The common view among Christians is that prophecy is about predicting the future. If you go to the prophecy section of your local Christian bookstore, you will find the *Left Behind* series of books by LaHaye and Jenkins and a whole host of books like them. The trouble is, these books are not prophetic in the biblical sense of the term. *Biblical prophecy is not focused on foretelling the future; rather, it declares the truth in the name of the Lord.* Books such as the *Left Behind* series stimulate a craving for intrigue and mystery and the bizarre. Speculating about the rapture and a one-world government headed by the anti-Christ is much more "fun" than the deep work of following Jesus. This work is summed up by prophetic voices such as Micah and James: "act justly, love mercy, walk humbly with your God" (Micah 6:8) and "look after orphans and widows in their distress and keep yourselves from being polluted by the world" (James 1:27). True prophecy frees up God's people to see reality clearly and challenges them to follow Jesus more deeply.

Prophetic vision seeks first the kingdom in every way. Prophetic vision (to use an analogy from the previous chapter) means recognizing which messages are being tuned into on our "radio receivers" and intentionally seeking to strengthen the "God" messages and to tune out the others. Ponder the words *normal* and *successful* for a moment. What does it mean to be a normal or a successful person? Prophetic living recognizes that how we define the terms *normal/abnormal* and *success/failure* depends entirely on which "radio stations" have the most powerful frequencies in our lives. The voice that is allowed to tell us what normal means and what success looks like is the voice that functions as our god. Prophecy—declaring the truth—is about challenging "normal" ways of seeing the world by naming instead a Godly kingdom perspective on seeing reality.

Let me give you an example: I have two friends in very different life situations. Both are college graduates. One of them is the chief executive officer of a software company who earns millions of dollars a year. He is very good at what he does and is widely respected in his field. Another friend works in a home for emotionally troubled teenagers; these teens verbally abuse her in a variety of ways and occasionally hurt her physically. She is patient and firm with them. She barely earns enough to live on in the big city where she works. Both of these people are using their gifts in productive ways. One of them earns more than 100 times the annual salary of the other one. That difference doesn't surprise us at all. That is *normal* in our world. This is also a way of saying that the work of the one is worth one hundred times as much as the work of the other, or, in other words, that computer software is one hundred times more valuable than struggling teenagers. One of these people is considered to be very *successful* by our society's standards, the other just barely so. A prophetic, truth-walking vision points out that this salary contrast is utterly bizarre and strange. Inside the kingdom of God, this difference in salary makes no sense at all. Inside the kingdom of mammon, it appears perfectly normal.

It's striking that very little about Jesus was considered to be normal. In Mark 3, we find the stunning account of how Jesus's mother Mary and his brothers thought that he was going insane. Mark writes, "Then Jesus entered a house, and again a crowd gathered, so that he and his disciples were not even able to eat. When his family heard about this, they went to take charge of him, for they said, 'he is out of his mind'" (Mark 3:20–21). They wanted to lock him up away from public view! In their eyes, Jesus wasn't normal; he didn't fit into the vision that shaped their lives and the life of their culture. Eventually they realized that Jesus was called to live a "seek-first-the-kingdom" life in all that he was and did. By living prophetically and walking in the truth, he completely redefined what it means to be normal and successful.

Well, it's easy to say that we need prophetic vision, but we have a problem. Scripture makes clear that prophets get murdered, even crucified. If they aren't murdered, they are shut down in some other way. Persecution happened throughout Scripture, and it still happens today. In North America, rather than murdering our prophets, we drown them out or dismiss them with a "whatever" shoulder shrug. "I hear you, you can say what you want, it even sounds kind of interesting, but it's not worth my time to ponder or engage, and it certainly isn't going to change me in any way. Whatever." "Whatever" is a powerful word; it shuts down prophetic voices and discourages prophetic living.

So, what does prophetic vision look like? Prophetic vision leads to being-sanctified, born-again living, that is, life that follows a pattern of dying and rising to new life. The old way of sin is slowly dying off and the new way of the Spirit is slowly growing stronger. Prophetic living embraces this pattern in the following ways:

1. *Blindness dies as an observant spirit comes to life.* Our culture breeds a type of fast-paced nervousness inside our brains that causes spiritual blindness, but the prophetic mind-set breeds an observant people, people who ponder slowly and carefully. Pondering is slow-motion reflecting, turning around and inside out, allowing the deeper realities below the surface to emerge. Such pondering allows the skill of *discernment*—truly seeing what lives beneath the surface—to grow.

2. *Conformity dies as a risk-taking, rebellious spirit comes to life.* The apostle Paul writes, "Do not be conformed any longer to the pattern of this world, but be transformed by the renewing of your mind" (Romans 12:2). While our culture encourages conformity, the prophetic mind-set encourages rebellious risk-taking. Christians reject the "normal" assumptions concerning career decisions, what money is spent on, on what basis people are valued, how leisure time is spent, why relationships are important. Rejecting conformity and redefining what is normal and successful according to the priorities of the kingdom of God transforms Christians into rebels, rebelling against falsity in the name of the Lord. Sometimes it's difficult to know what "transformed normal" looks like, so living in this way requires the freedom to move with trial and error. The way of obedience is the way of risk-taking.

3. *Individualism dies as an encouraging, communal spirit comes to life.* Whereas our culture breeds pseudocommunity that revolves around guessing who will emerge victorious on the latest reality TV show or this year's Super Bowl, the prophetic mind-set requires true community: a community in which prophets speak and hearers listen. Worship is God's greatest gift to us to cultivate the prophetic mind-set, to give us a medium in which we can begin to share observations, ponder, discern, encourage, and be challenged to take risks as a community. Our culture tells us that worship should make us feel good, but biblically driven prophetic

worship wakes us up and places us on the painfully liberating path of being taken from death to new life, of walking in the truth.

Truth-Walking Habits

A few years ago, two Christian college students carried out a course assignment in a unique and creative way: armed with a camcorder and a clipboard, they walked around their campus and asked students six trivia questions, three dealing with television commercials and three dealing with Scripture. The resulting video demonstrated that most students knew commercial trivia much better than biblical trivia. Though at first shocking, on second thought this is not a surprising discovery. The average North American sees a million television commercials in a lifetime. The average Christian does not spend as much time with Scripture. "Americans revere the Bible," says pollster George Gallup Jr., "but by and large they don't read it." The habits that shape our lives are generally much more conducive to immersion in consumer culture than to immersion in the story of God recorded in Scripture.

There's an old proverb that says, "If you're not making plans of your own, you're part of someone else's." Our society has plans for us that resonate with its idolatrous goals, plans that encourage spending more, doing more for the sake of one's country, and living by instincts and feelings rather than commitments. Growing in sanctification involves dying to the plans of others and living inside the plans of the Lord. Prophetic living grows as a community engages in prophetic habits: regular, ongoing, communal activities that say yes to the coming of the kingdom and no to the god-denying dynamics of the culture around us. These habits lie at the heart of our sanctification, and they deepen the colors of life.

Let's think about the word *habits* for a moment. Does it have good, bad, or neutral connotations for you? When I was a young adult, the word definitely had bad connotations for me and my generation. We perceived habits as the things our parents did routinely without thinking about them, without any sense of commitment, without any passion. If going to church is just a habit, we thought, then we shouldn't go. Recently I heard a teenager say, "Most people don't really want to go to church— they go just because it's a habit and they think they're supposed to." Perhaps times haven't changed.

Might the word also have positive connotations? Walk through a typical day for a moment and examine how many habits are part of the day. I tend to get up at more or less the same time every morning, take a shower, have breakfast with my family, spend some time in devotions, go to work, greet my colleagues with almost exactly the same words every day, and so on. My day is filled with dozens of habits. These habits are very liberating because they free me from having to make decisions about every single thing that I do. I don't have to decide "What time shall I wake up?" "Do I really need a shower today?" "Shall I eat breakfast?" "Do I need to do devotions?" "Shall I go to work today?" Many parts of my day are "predecided," as it were, by regular habits that I follow day by day. They may vary from time to time, but the general pattern frees me up to focus on other things. Habits are God's gift to us to give shape to our lives.

The Lord also sees habits as central to the pattern of becoming more mature in Christ, to help us daily die and rise to new life in Christ. Consider Colossians 3:16, where Paul writes, "Let the word of Christ dwell in you richly as you teach and admonish one another with all wisdom and as you sing Psalms, hymns and spiritual songs with gratitude in your hearts to God." The word *habit* is not found in this verse, but its concept is present in two different ways that flow from the connection between the words *habit* and *inhabit*. The word *inhabit* means to dwell in. The word *habit* means a regular, ongoing practice. These words seem utterly disconnected from one another. But let me read that verse again using these two words: "Let the word of Christ *inhabit* you richly as you practice these two *habits*: first, teaching and admonishing one another with all wisdom, and second, singing Psalms, hymns and spiritual songs with gratitude in your hearts to God." Here is the point: through the Holy Spirit, Jesus Christ comes to live within us, to inhabit us. But we must *make room* for the Holy Spirit to dwell within, and the biblical manner for making such room is to practice habits that make space for God.

From beginning to end, the Scriptures are a covenantal book, and *covenant* means (among other things) that we are God's partners. In a life of partnership, God's promises and our response are completely interwoven. God desires to dwell within us, but we must sing that Christmas chorus every day: "Let every heart prepare him room." This covenantal character means that our habits are part of an ongoing cycle of action: God makes promises to be with us; we respond to those promises in a variety of ways that include regular habits; these habits expand space for God's presence to move among and within us, and God dwells within us "more richly"; and so the covenantal cycle continues. *This cycle requires action on our part; engaging in regular habits is a central way in which we encourage God's work of maturing us in Christ.*

Some say that a habit such as going to worship every Sunday is silly because often we can't identify precisely what the benefit was from our hour of participation. Perhaps we can't, and that's because a habit is an *act of faith*. There is no proof, no rational guarantee that habits will have any significant result. But the act of faith is this: if we engage in a regular habit, then we will gradually—over time—make space for God to dwell among us through the Holy Spirit. I love the way the writer of Ecclesiastes expresses this truth:

> As you do not know the path of the wind or how a baby is formed in a mother's womb, so you cannot understand the

work of God, the maker of all things. Sow your seed in the morning and at evening let not your hands be idle, for you do not know which will succeed, whether this or that, or whether both will do equally well. (Ecclesiastes 11:5–6)

Be faithfully regular in your work, he writes, not because it guarantees success, but rather because you *do not know* what guarantees success. Be faithful, and leave it to God to do *his work* through *your work*. God's eternal faithfulness works through our regular faithfulness.

Truth-walking habits are always grounded in faith and hope. We are called to *trust* that our actions will be blessed by the presence of the Spirit of God.

Examples and Characteristics of Truth-Walking Habits

To make this notion more concrete, here is a list of habits that give shape to the Christian life:

- being knowledgeable about the affairs of our world
- eating together with others
- praying (alone and with others)
- publicly naming injustice and evil for what they really are
- supporting and encouraging others who do such public naming
- giving of our time and money
- lovingly caring for God's creation in every way that we can
- seeking out and encouraging the struggling
- practicing solitude
- studying Scripture (both alone and with others)
- passing on the wisdom of God to the next generation
- participating in communal worship events

- playing with others
- taking Sabbath rest (daily, weekly, and for longer periods at certain times of the year)

Just as sanctification covers every area of our life and our identity, so there are habits that give expression to every part of our walk with God. Some are daily, some weekly, some only annually, some quite random. Each of these habits is an example of living out Ecclesiastes 11:6, of sowing seed in the morning and of not being idle in the evening, for we do not know which will succeed.

Let me give you some examples of how habits create space for God in a world that seeks to shut him out.

The habit of sharing meals together is a declining habit in our culture. There are many reasons for this, including: (1) we're increasingly too busy to be able to find a common time during which we can share a meal; (2) the commercial world has recognized this problem, so that the number of fast-food outlets in North America has doubled in the last generation, allowing people an easy solution to the problem of finding a common mealtime; (3) for those who prefer to eat at home, the microwave has enabled a family to eat the same food but at different times, because it is extremely convenient to quickly heat something up and eat individually; (4) even when people do eat together, it has become increasingly common that this shared meal occurs in front of a television set, so the television becomes the glue that bonds the eaters together.

Eating is a habitation of the Holy Spirit, in other words, a habit that makes room for the Spirit to inhabit. Preparing a meal is an art that takes the fruits of God's creation and works with them in such a way that both the human body and the human spirit are nourished. People who sit around a table together interact with each other, and, even if the discussion has moments of anger and frustration, there is meaningful and important interaction going on. Eating together points to the wholeness of life: there are dimensions of artistry, hospitality, and loving others all interwoven with the act of eating. Sharing food is one of the most basic ways of giving and receiving love with thanksgiving. Eating properly requires time and forces people to "waste time together," as it were, and, to thrive, relationships require wasting time together. Many Christian traditions have connected eating together with devotional times, and the connection is natural and obvious. As the food binds us together and nourishes us in many different ways, so Scripture and prayer also nourish us and bind us together.

But this picture sounds a bit romanticized, right? Our family's mealtimes may include arguments, people rushing through their food, a lack of thankfulness, and, when it gets to devotional time, phrases like, "Everybody be quiet—hurry up and read the Bible passage," and "That Bible story again? We had that in Sunday school last month." Can this be called a habit that encourages the inhabitation of the Holy Spirit? Or is it an outdated annoyance that could easily be let go and replaced with fast food and microwaved meals?

I'm not ready to let this habit go. In a culture in which we become increasingly disconnected from each other and from the bounty of God's creation, eating good meals together is a vital lifeline, a prophetic yes to the kingdom of God. I know of churches that practice a family night once a week that begins with a potluck meal and continues with church education and youth programs. I know of Bible study groups who share a meal together once a month. That great sacrament, the Lord's Supper, is based on the habit of eating together as a community.

Let's ponder two other truth-walking habits: fasting and keeping Sabbath. These are two different habits, but they have this element in common: both fasting and keeping Sabbath are ways of saying no to routines of everyday life. Fasting is a voluntary letting go of a part of daily life for a short time, most commonly associated with eating food. Sabbath refers to taking a time of rest from one's daily labor. Our cell-phone- and Internet-driven world is a place that breaks down boundaries and rhythms of life; both Sabbath and fasting are boundary-setting, rhythm-establishing habits. Yes, work has the tendency to invade my entire being and my entire life, but I will set this boundary as a way of declaring, "My work does not rule me. My identity is not focused on my work."

Fasting is a form of self-denial, a foregoing of a regular activity in one's life. Most commonly, fasting is associated with food because food is a life necessity and historically humankind has become anxious about the necessities of life. Fasting is a way of saying, "I will not focus on my anxiety about receiving the necessities of life, I will trust in the Lord." Fasting reminds us that we "do not live on bread alone, but on every word that comes from the mouth of God" (Matthew 4:4). In the context of an affluent society in which very few worry about finding enough food, a society that becomes anxious about the quantity, speed, and pervasiveness of life in an electronic world, fasting takes on a whole new meaning. There is wisdom in fasting in a variety of new ways: fasting from watching TV, fasting from sending and checking e-mail, fasting from the telephone, fasting from the automobile for any trips of less than a mile, and so on.

One final, brief example. I often ask my students to write a short reflection on what has shaped their faith life. One young man wrote the following: "When I was twelve, our family bought a ping-pong table, and I would play with my dad three or four times a week for fifteen minutes or so each time. We did this until I finished high school and left for college. It seemed like just a bit of recreation that we did, but now I recognize that those times playing ping-pong served to keep me connected with my dad during a time in life when that is difficult to do. We didn't talk much as we played, but because we played we were able to talk a lot more when we needed to." Isn't that beautiful? That's a truth-walking habit in action, playing together and creating space for connection.

These habits come in many shapes and sizes. In a culture where mindless absorption of hours of television and video is increasingly common, not owning a TV or placing significant restrictions on the use of one's TV can be a truth-walking habit. The manner in which we celebrate Christmas, birthdays, and other special events provide opportunities for habits that celebrate relationships and events instead of succumbing to guilt-driven consumerism. Each of these habits is actually a prophetic practice that expands space for God because each of these habits says yes to the kingdom of God and is also an act of rebellion that says no to the idols of our culture.

Habit Clusters

Truth-walking habits cover every area of our being-sanctified lives, so we might say that "habit clusters" guide our sanctification. This clustering is important because habits are *mutually reinforcing*, that is, the practice of one habit makes it easier to practice another.

For example, a friend of mine told me that she had always disliked change; she wanted her life to be orderly and under control. She practiced the habit of Sunday worship, and at one point a particular sermon that she heard was about allowing the Lord to stretch us out of our comfort zones. That same week, she learned of a Russian exchange student who suddenly needed a home for a year. It struck her that there was a connection between the sermon and the need; she recognized that providing a home for this high school student would conflict with her desires for an orderly life, but she and her husband decided that opening their home to this young lady was the right thing to do. The habit of Sunday worship led to a growth in the habit of hospitality. After a wonderful year with this student in their home, the habit of hospitality had stretched their hearts in such a way that this couple decided to adopt a Romanian child. Because following Jesus is a "unified whole," the habits that we practice strengthen each other.

That adoption story comes at the end of a *sequential* habit cluster, that is, A leads to B, which leads to C. Habit clusters also work simultaneously, because the Christian life is shaped by multiple habits. Janine volunteers once a week at the Family Crisis Center, worships every Sunday, and plays penny poker with three other friends most Thursday evenings. Her experiences at the FCC have strengthened her awareness of how messed up life can get and how difficult it is for those who have experienced the worst of these messes to cope. As she brings those experiences to Sunday worship, she is struck by how many hymns that she has sung for years refer to broken, needy people, and she wonders why she had never noticed that before. She also notices that the conversations around the card table on Thursdays are getting deeper; as she tells some of her FCC stories there, other friends add in their own stories, and the relationships grow deeper as the cards are shuffled. Each of these three habits strengthens the other two, and Janine grows as a more sturdy tree in the kingdom of God.

But what about this problem of doing things habitually without passion? Isn't that a form of hypocrisy? I believe there's another way of understanding this phenomenon. A culture that preaches "if it feels good, do it" cannot understand why regular habits have an important role to play in life because regularity means that *I do it whether I feel like it or not.* Habits are a way of saying that our actions are guided by our *commitments* rather than our *feelings,* and the habit sustains the commitment during those times when the feelings are dry and the passion is dormant. Thus, habits say no to placing feelings at the center and yes to commitment. Or, to put it another way, habits serve to keep our gardens well watered and weeded until Spirit-shaped, being-sanctified feelings are able to grow there again.

The word *habit* often carries connotations of unchanging tradition, but a key to practicing prophetic habits is that they are flexible and adapt to changing circumstances. The father of the twelve-year-old boy bought a ping-pong table because he recognized that his son was entering adolescence and new family habits would be needed to help them navigate that particular journey. Many congregations that I am familiar with are struggling with the necessity of having a second worship service on Sunday. Is this a declining habit? Is it declining because worshipers are maturing so deeply in Christ they don't need it, or because the too-busy dynamics of our culture have weakened our commitment to this habit, or some of each? On the other hand, in the last fifteen years we have seen a dramatic rise in small group ministry in all denominations. Why has this habit come to be seen as so important now? Could it be a way of maturing in Christ by building community in the midst of the community-breaking dynamics of our fast-paced world?

How do we know which habits to practice and how to practice them so that we create space for God and allow the word of Christ to dwell in us richly? Part of living in the Spirit is that we are not given a simple recipe for how to pattern our lives within godly habits. Rather, we are called to understand the needs of our situation and to construct habits that we believe will make space for God. Because our situations constantly change, our habits need to be revisited and revised. We cannot worship in exactly the same way we did fifty years ago. Family habits today cannot be identical to those of a generation or two ago.

Problems with Habits

Because we aren't given a recipe for prophetic living, we know that we are going to get it wrong sometimes. Eugene Peterson, a wise and respected Christian author known best for his Bible translation *The Message,* tells the following story from his childhood. One November, his mother stumbled across a verse in Jeremiah chastising the people of Israel for bowing down to sacred trees. Immediately she concluded that Christmas trees were a sacrilege, and never again did one enter their home. Reflecting as an adult, Peterson concluded that his mother had engaged in shoddy biblical interpretation, but at the same time she taught her family something vitally important about the Christian life. She taught them that following Jesus requires a pattern of saying no and saying yes. In other words, even if we get the habits wrong, the act of seeking to find the right prophetic patterns in itself is a crucial part of the process. Of course, misguided attempts to establish prophetic patterns can be damaging, but Peterson's story is encouraging, especially when the fear of getting everything just right paralyzes Christians.

The place of habits in the Christian life will always contain distortions. We will be tempted by works righteousness, concluding that God owes us something because we are following him so faithfully. We will be tempted by empty ritualism, going through the motions just to look good before others and before God. At times, habits may become an obsessive addiction so that we are unable to be flexible in our practice of them and they become bonds that constrict us rather than windows to the Holy Spirit. All of these temptations may lead us to become discouraged or cynical, and they may lead us to want to abandon regular habits entirely.

Probably the greatest danger that arises from the practice of habits is legalism. We are easily tempted to transform our habits into commandments by which we judge others and ourselves. Legalism simply means that we place laws at the center of our lives and use them to measure our own worth and the worth of others; in other words, *our identity is determined by what we do.* "I am a good person because I attend church; finish my homework; treat the opposite sex with respect; don't drink, smoke, or swear; and pray every day. She is a bad person because she goes out drinking every Thursday night, misses far too many early morning classes, and flirts shamelessly with those loose guys." These two sentences contain long lists of habits, which are used to determine the worth of two human beings. That's legalism, which always leads to judgmentalism.

Remember the radio receiver analogy? To be a Christian is to seek to be tuned in to that station that declares "nothing can separate us from the love of God that is ours in Christ Jesus our Lord." God declares that I am loved, that I am worthwhile, because of Jesus and not because of the habits that I practice. It's actually one of those *other* radio stations—one of the lying ones—that broadcasts, "Your worth—and everyone else's—is determined by how you live." The habits that we practice are our way of saying back to God, "Thank you for loving us so deeply through Jesus Christ. Please accept our simple habits as our sacrifice to you, our way of seeking to make our lives a stronger, deeper home for you to inhabit." It's easy to write these words, but every Christian that I know (including me) has difficulty living out the distinction between habit-shaped living and legalism. Such struggles are inevitable in the sanctified life; we must be aware of them and plug on as well as we can, "sowing our seed in the morning." We are not called to be perfect; we are called to be faithful.

In addition to these distortions in our efforts to practice prophetic habits, we also practice bad habits that serve only to undermine the Spirit's sanctifying work. Getting hooked on mindless TV programming, addictive computer games, superficial and demeaning conversational patterns with friends, shoddy study habits, junk food, racial slurs, and so on also become habitual and therefore become part of who we are. Part of the work of developing truth-walking habits includes recognizing and saying no to those habits that weaken us.

Developing Truth-Walking Habits

Most of us experienced a drastic change in the habit patterns of life after we graduated from high school. If we went on to college, we soon discovered that the patterns of college life are quite different from the patterns of high school. In college, there may be large blocks of unscheduled time during the day, the living situation changes from a family home to a dormitory, and meals occur in a cafeteria rather than the dining room. In addition, there are no parents around to oversee the habits of coming in at night, eating, doing schoolwork, attending church, and so on. Habits that once were (at least partially) supervised by others now become a matter of personal decision. These changes are monumental, and transitioning through them well is crucial for one's spiritual maturation. This transition is hampered by the antihabit nature of our culture; a spirit that says "I'll do what I feel like when I feel like it" undermines the practice of strong, truth-walking habits. Recognizing the need to make commitments and learn skills helps one overcome these challenges.

Making Accountable Commitments

A habit is almost automatic—we do it without thinking about it. Every morning after breakfast, I write in a devotional journal for fifteen minutes. The time is open, I have a quiet room, I'm used to the pattern, and it's quite easy to keep the habit alive. Some days the writing is more meaningful than on other days, but that doesn't matter. The habit continues, and it's not that difficult to keep it going.

Starting a new habit—or continuing an old habit when the circumstances of our lives change—is much more challenging. Often it requires a very intentional decision to make an accountable commitment. The opportunity to make commitments is one of the Lord's great gifts to us, because a commitment is like a gift that keeps on giving. A commitment is a way of saying, "I will do this because it flows from who I am," and then the living out of that commitment strengthens who I am. For example, my commitment to devotional journaling arises from my conviction that the Lord has called me to be a reflective, prayerful person who is more and more aware of his presence in my life at all times. The habit I practice based on that conviction helps me to grow in prayerful reflectiveness. Habits that encourage sanctification begin with commitments.

Because we encounter so many antihabit pressures, allowing ourselves to be held accountable by others is very helpful. Adding a habit to our lives is a bit like grafting a branch onto a tree—it's not natural! The grafted branch is surrounded by tape to hold it in place until the natural connections to the tree develop and the fasteners are no longer necessary. Habit accountability is like that tape. During my third year of college, I realized that I wasn't getting enough physical exercise so I decided to run two miles three times a week. The trouble was, I never felt like running. A friend of mine agreed that he needed more exercise too, so we agreed to run together every other day at 4 P.M. Because I knew that he would be waiting for me at our starting point, I was there every time. We held each other accountable. Habits that involve two or more people easily lend themselves to accountability. Habits that are best practiced alone may need an accountability partner or a small group where regular "check-ups" occur.

Learning Skills

Living prophetically requires *skill,* and every truth-walking habit also involves learning specific skills. A skill refers to an activity that one has learned to perform well. The easiest area of life to see this process at work is in sports. Playing basketball requires acquiring skills in free throw shooting, passing, dunking, making a variety of different shots, anticipating the flow of the play, and so on. Each one of the skills involved in playing basketball requires different techniques to be done well. A well-rounded player aims to master the set of skills through years of hard work and paying attention to good coaching. Similarly, practicing strong habits requires developing competency in a variety of skills.

Take, for example, the habit of encouraging a struggling person. This habit would involve the following skills:

(1) *Being able to notice when someone is struggling.* Most folks don't wear their struggles on their sleeves for all the world to see. We are taught at an early age to pretend that we're fine most of the time. Yet most of us are not superb actors, and we tend to drop many little hints if we're having a particularly difficult time. The habit of encouragement begins by cultivating the skill of noticing, of being able to put the hints together to realize that someone is in need of encouragement.

(2) *Knowing whether I am the right person to provide encouragement at this time.* Some people are able to receive encouraging words from us, others are not. Some will be angry and embarrassed when we tell them that we've noticed that they are struggling. Others will breathe a sigh of relief and be thankful that someone understands and cares. Providing encouragement always involves a risk; know-

ing whether I am the right person and whether now is the right time require skills of discernment.

(3) *Knowing what to say and what not to say.* Dozens of times, I have heard people say, "I want to encourage my friend, but I don't know what to say!" What words provide encouragement, what words free a person to speak to us about difficult matters, and what words shut down a conversation? What sorts of body language and eye contact convey love and understanding? Choosing encouraging words and learning how to listen are central skills for this particular habit.

How does one learn these skills? Truth-walking habits are learned through three interrelated ways: doing them, seeing others model them, and being coached in them (just as in sports). The "doing" helps one recognize what to look for in watching others; both of these awaken an awareness of the need for coaching; coaching provides encouragement and guidance for continued "doing," and so the wheel goes round.

Let's go back to the habit of encouraging others. The first step in learning is to "just do it." Every professional hockey player began by lacing on skates as a three-year-old and falling flat on his butt dozens of times. Learning new habits works exactly the same way. We learn best from our successes and mistakes, and it's a slow process. A three-year-old doesn't lace up his first pair of skates and take on the Colorado Avalanche. No, he holds his father's hand while skating loops at the local ice rink. Learning to be an encourager starts the same way.

Second, we remember how we have seen others provide encouragement. Parents, teachers, and friends tried to encourage us, and we remember which things were helpful and which ones were simply annoying. We remember seeing a teacher discretely pull someone else aside during class, quietly offering a few words of encouragement in the middle of a busy room. Our own trial-and-error attempts at providing encouragement help us to recall the models we've seen in the past.

Third, we seek to be taught so that we will continue to grow. As we seek to practice encouragement, we find ourselves dealing with increasingly more difficult and complicated struggles. College students regularly come into the offices of counselors and professors to ask for advice: "My roommate is really struggling with [loneliness, depression, parental issues, sexual issues], and I want to help him, but I'm not sure what to say. Do you have any advice?" These three ways of learning are all mutually reinforcing: the doing makes you more observant of models, and it gives you more courage to ask others to teach you the required skills. This three-part pattern of learning skills applies to *all* of the habits that are part of the being-sanctified life.

Perhaps you are thinking, "Attending Sunday worship is a very important habit, but I wouldn't call it *a skill*. I just show up on Sunday morning, do what the liturgy tells me to do, sit there and listen." Not so. Participating in congregational worship is just as demanding as any other habit in the Christian life and requires the active learning and intentional practice of just as many skills. These skills include the following:

(1) *Allowing one's hunger for the Lord to be freed up so we can receive the nourishment that worship provides.* Hunger for God is not automatic! Sometimes it takes hard work to wake it up!

(2) *Learning to bring all of one's being before the face of God.* Someone told me once that when he walks into church on Sunday morning, he leaves 80 percent of himself in the car in the parking lot. It's a challenge to bring "all of me" into the pew.

(3) *Learning to see the presence of God through very human words that are spoken or sung.* The mystery of worship is that God is present there! But that presence comes to us through the words and actions of human beings. I remember listening to a preacher during my high school years who had a nervous tic. My friends and I

spent the entire service counting the number of times we saw the tic (yes, I know, a real teenage thing to do). Needless to say, we did not recognize the presence of God in that worship service.

(4) *Coming to experience the fellowship of the saints with a body full of sinners.* There's an old poem that goes: "Oh to dwell above with saints we love, that will be glory. But to dwell below with saints we know, that's a different story." It takes skilled prophetic vision to recognize the body of Christ in those broken, ordinary folks with whom we worship every week.

(5) *Learning to gather strength from centuries-old traditions of Christian worship.* The worship wars between contemporary and traditional fans tend to obscure the fact that biblical worship is always both contemporary and traditional. Worshipers seeking relevant, contemporary nourishment receive this with much more depth when they recognize the wonderful benefits passed on to us by the saints of yesteryear.

(6) *Understanding how all of the different components of worship are designed to lead God's people into his presence.* Worship involves various rhythms and sequences; certain hymns are more appropriate for the beginning, others for the ending. Traveling inside these rhythms is improved as we recognize the road map that we are following.

In other words, worship is not automatic! It, too, requires that we learn the necessary skills by doing, by observing others, and by being taught.

Is this whole process starting to sound somewhat "heavy"—this maturing in Christ through a three-step process of learning habits? It's not as overwhelming as it sounds. If you examine your life, you will probably notice multiple examples of habit learning, though you may not have thought about them in those terms. All of our lives are shaped by many habits, and growing in Christ in this way is not so much a radical change as it is a refinement of something that is already there. Furthermore, we are not called to suddenly take on fifteen new habits and become highly skilled superstars. The Christian life is about growing inch by inch like a tree; it's about becoming intentional, developing and honing our skills. There's a dimension of playfully serious experimentation woven into our maturation that asks questions like, "I wonder what it would be like to fast from e-mail (or TV or chocolate) one day per week—would that affect my walk with God in any way?" "It seems like I'm always too busy to keep in touch with a good friend. Why don't we plan to go for hot chocolate every Wednesday evening for an hour?" "Would getting up half an hour earlier on Sundays for quiet reflection prepare me more adequately for worship?" Growing in the practice of truth-walking habits is best done one habit at a time.

Developing a Truth-Walking Community

Practicing truth-walking habits is not just an individual activity, you in your small corner and I in mine; we practice many of them as communities. Habits are almost always communal in character. Worship, encouraging conversations, speaking out against injustice, eating together—these are all activities that involve *groups* of people, and thus habits are community-forming. Even those habits that are personal and individual, such as Bible reading, praying, going for walks alone, and writing in a journal, are acts that make us *more fit to be in community*. Truth-walking habits are a way of saying yes to the body of Christ and no to the community fragmentation that is so prevalent today. Sanctification is both personal and communal, and our habits address both of these dimensions. Our churches, our homes, our schools, our friendships, all of the organizations and activities that reflect our Christian commitment, are called to say yes to the coming of the kingdom and no to the God-denying dynamics of this age. Do you belong to a truth-walking church? Is your home a place that says yes to the kingdom and no to the spirits of this world? How can churches, homes, dorms, friendship groups, and classrooms possibly walk in the truth more fully?

To answer this, we need to go back to an earlier theme: the definitions of success and normalcy. Our culture frequently defines success and normalcy in terms of dollars or hits per day or speed or audience share or public acceptance—the list goes on. In the kingdom of God, success and normalcy are defined in terms of *whom you are following.* If you are walking in the same direction as Jesus, then it doesn't matter if you lose everything you own and if others despise you as a loser and a wimp; you are, in the true sense, both normal and successful.

The same holds true of our communities. As a community takes tiny steps in the right direction, it becomes a truth-walking community. God's kingdom comes through millions of tiny steps in the right direction and through millions of cups of cold water given in Jesus's name. And each step in the right direction creates the possibility of bigger steps to build on that step.

Let me give you two examples to illustrate this truth, one from Scripture and one from recent history.

Situation #1: Acts 6–9. The Holy Spirit has been poured out upon the church in Jerusalem, and a vibrant body is formed that worships together in homes, teaches one another, eats together, and makes sure that no one is in need. But there are growing pains in this large body. During its first years, the church is comprised entirely of Jews, but some are Aramaic-speaking Jews and some are Greek-speaking Jews. There are inter-ethnic tensions between these two groups, and the Greek-speaking widows are not getting their fair share of the food. After this matter is brought to the attention of the church leaders, they conclude that this is an important matter, but, being too busy themselves, they appoint seven Greek-speaking men to minister to the Greek-speaking widows.

Here we see a wonderful truth-walking habit (caring for the poor) hampered by the sin of ethnic/linguistic pride. The early church responded with a small step of faithfulness: in a church numbering thousands of believers, they appointed a tiny group of seven men to deal with the problem. It was a way of saying no to the ethnically divided world and yes to the kingdom.

Now, trace with me the consequences of this tiny step. These Greek-speaking men are not as engrained in the Jewish traditions as the others; they have a bit of an outsider perspective on matters. They have been appointed to care for the poor, but one of them, Stephen, is a very gifted speaker, and his wisdom and oratory gifts come to the attention of the Jewish leaders. They become angry with him, accusing him of speaking against the ways of Moses.

At his defense trial, Stephen delivers a sermon to the Sanhedrin. Though unfinished, it is the longest sermon recorded in the book of Acts, and it is the defining sermon of the early church. In it, Stephen makes two radical points: first, he shows how Christianity is rooted in the Old Testament, and second, he demonstrates how it departs from Old Testament traditions in significant ways. The Sanhedrin recognizes how radical Stephen's statements are and, in a fit of irrational rage, they drag him out of the city and stone him.

Two important results flow from this stoning. First, believers flee for their lives: the church is scattered from Jerusalem and the message of the gospel is spread throughout Samaria and north to Damascus. Second, Luke makes a special point of telling us that Saul is there when Stephen is stoned to death (Acts 8:1). Saul hears Stephen's final sermon. He continues the persecution, but, on his way to Damascus, the Lord claims him as his apostle to the Gentiles. And here's what is so interesting: there are striking similarities between Saul's (Paul's) epistles and Stephen's final sermon. Stephen's Greek-speaking perspective on the Old Testament is carried over and developed by Saul, now named Paul, as he becomes the Lord's chief representative to the Greek-speaking world, to the Gentiles. And then the church spreads throughout the entire Roman Empire and up into Europe.

Obviously, history is much more complex than this simple account gives credit for. But, according to the book of Acts, a direct sequence of events flows from the early church's habit of caring for the poor to the conversion of Saul and his missionary journeys throughout the Roman empire. A little step in the right direction creates space for the next step and the next step; space is made for the Spirit to move, and the mission of the church is furthered.

Situation #2: More recent history. In the 1980s, a small group of believers met for weekly prayer in a church in Leipzig, East Germany. Among other things, they prayed for the fall of the Communist government there. Week after week they met, offering their seemingly futile prayers. Toward the end of the eighties, these prayer meetings started to grow dramatically in number. Eventually there were thousands gathered outside that church, peacefully saying no to the communist government. These prayer demonstrations spread to other cities in East Germany, and, combined with other historical forces, contributed to the fall of the Communist government and the reunification of the German nation. A half-dozen people gathering for a weekly prayer—a simple habit practiced in faith—contributed to an earthshaking change.

A truth-walking community is characterized by two ingredients: the flexibility to take tiny steps in the right direction and the patience to wait in faith as these steps are used by God. Most of our tiny steps will not have such earth-shattering consequences. There are thousands of prayer groups around the world that meet faithfully, and their regular meetings do not lead to stunning newspaper headlines. But it doesn't matter. We sow our seed in the morning and at evening we do not let our hands be idle, and we do not know which will succeed. That is the way of truth-walking obedience.

Conclusion: Deepening the Colors

To be a Christian is to be a house, a temple, under construction. Most of our dwellings are functional: that is, they are designed to allow us to work, sleep, relax, relate to others, and do the things that one must do in a home. When we imagine God constructing us into a house, perhaps we imagine that God is making us functional, too, maturing us so that we can serve him more fully.

But God's work is so much richer than functionality or usefulness. He is constructing something of exquisite beauty. I imagine that when the Lord looks at his children now, he sees the faint beginnings of our New Jerusalem jewel colors beginning to take shape, beginning to deepen in vitality and richness. As children of Adam and Eve come to the cross to receive the gift of salvation, as they surrender to the Holy Spirit and mature in Christ, and as they long for the fullness of all things when the entire cosmos is made new, the colors continue to deepen. When the communion of saints prays "Thy kingdom come" and tries to embody "seek first the kingdom" in a thousand different ways, the colors continue to deepen. When the body of believers practices dozens of different habits that say yes to the reign of the Lamb and no to the spirits of this world, the colors continue to deepen. Sometimes they even become deep enough—just for a few moments—to glimpse the faint outlines of one of the jewels that John saw in his vision. Those glimpses make us long even more intensely for the completed city to be revealed, and we pray, "Amen, come Lord Jesus" (Revelation 22:20).

Chapter Five

Our Lives—

Stories in Progress

Transformed by the Holy Spirit

Is the Holy Spirit living inside you? How do you know? Just where is he? What is he doing? Is he inside you more at some times than at others? Is he ever absent? Is the Holy Spirit responsible for the "good" things that you do and say, and is the devil responsible for the "bad" things? Is it possible for you to shut down the Spirit and ignore his presence in your life?

There is so much mystery and misunderstanding surrounding the place of the Holy Spirit in the Christian life. Sometimes theologians refer to the Spirit as the "shyest" member of the Trinity because he does not like to draw attention to himself; he much prefers to point to Jesus and the Father, deepening our relationship with them. Jesus teaches his disciples that when the Holy Spirit comes, "he will bring glory to me by taking from what is mine and making it known to you" (John 16:14); he also says "when the Counselor comes, whom I will send to you from the Father, the Spirit of truth who goes out from the Father, he will testify about me" (John 15:26). This connection between the Spirit and Jesus is so strong that Paul dares to say, "I have been crucified with Christ and I no longer live, but Christ lives in me" (Galatians 2:20a). Through the Holy Spirit, we are so deeply connected to Jesus that we actually die with him and are resurrected with him *right now;* "since then, you have been raised with Christ, set your hearts on things above . . . for you died, and your life is now hidden with Christ in God" (Colossians 3:1, 3).

I have been crucified? I have been resurrected? Jesus lives within me through the Holy Spirit? Sometimes these biblical phrases seem so *unreal.* Jesus died on the cross, not me. Jesus rose from the grave, not me. His death and resurrection are the central defining events of the Christian faith—how can I die and be raised, too? But the Bible is very clear: through the Holy Spirit, our relationship to Jesus is so deep that we share in his death and resurrection. "Don't you know that all of us who were baptized into Christ Jesus were baptized into his death? We were therefore buried with him through baptism into death in order that, just as Christ was raised from the dead through the glory of the Father, we too may live a new life" (Romans 6:3–4).

The best word to describe how the Holy Spirit is working in our lives is *transformation.* Just as a caterpillar goes through a kind of "death" and comes to new life, transformed into a butterfly, so the Spirit puts our old self to death and we are born again in Christ as a new person. The caterpillar and the butterfly are the same creature, but the transformation is dramatic. Similarly, my "old self" and my "new self" are both "me," but a transformation is taking place from the first to the second. Paul describes this, too: "The Lord is the Spirit, and where the Spirit of the Lord is, there is freedom. And we . . . are being transformed into his likeness with ever-increasing glory, which comes from the Lord, who is the Spirit" (2 Corinthians 3:17–18).

In Chapter Two, I quoted C. S. Lewis's analogy that compares the Spirit's transforming work to a house undergoing extensive renovation. My wife and I have owned three different homes that were renovated. I remember with a smile one builder who sat down with us to discuss our plans and said, "Before we begin, I want to make sure that you have a strong marriage, because house renovation is always more complicated and takes longer than you think, and the stresses it brings can be hard on a marriage." We told him that we thought we could handle it (and we did!), but he was right: once you start knocking out walls and rerouting the plumbing, you discover things you couldn't know beforehand, and you have to readjust your understanding of the whole project.

The Christian life is like that, too. After we say to the Lord, "Renovate me, because I am yours. Do with me as you please," we can expect the unexpected, and it may "hurt abominably and not make sense," as Lewis says. Our *past* experiences help us to make sense of our lives, but God is growing us toward his *future* that we cannot fully understand. We can call the hurt that comes from the Spirit's renovation "growing pain," or, since we are being born again, "labor pain." That's why Paul writes, "We know that the whole creation has been groaning as in the pains of childbirth. . . . Not only so, but we ourselves, who have the first-fruits of the Spirit, groan inwardly as we wait eagerly for our adoption as sons" (Romans 8:22–23).

The hurt is also caused by spiritual warfare: my heart, my identity, is a battle zone. God has laid his claim upon my life, but other forces are reluctant to let go of their claims. The Christian life always involves identity competition: we are created to reflect God, but we often reflect other, false gods instead. Sorting out this identity competition is very complex and can be partly understood through a diagram that looks like this.

The three circles and five arrows work this way: God's word, truth, stands at the center of our understanding of reality. This word tells us the story of God and seeks to shape our identity and the identity of the entire Christian community as we live inside that story. The arrow from the center to the middle circle describes that shaping power. As we are born again day by day, putting to death our identities that are not rooted in God's word and growing in identities that are, that arrow is doing its powerful work. And, as a new people, we are called to be salt and light in the world around us, contagious with the work of God so that in countless ways his goodness flows through us to the culture around us. Whenever Christians are instruments who bring others to the Lord and further the growth of justice and mercy and healing in this broken world, that arrow has extended from the middle circle to the outer circle, spreading the goodness of God. Christians also encourage, strengthen, and challenge one another, helping each other to grow in the strength of the Lord. Therefore, we see a two-pointed arrow inside the middle circle.

But arrows move in the other direction as well. Our culture has a powerful shaping effect upon Christians. Sometimes it seems that the arrow flowing from the culture to the Christian community is more powerful than the one flowing the other way. The influence of North American materialism can easily be seen in the rampant consumerism present in the Christian community. The two-pointed arrow in the middle circle also has a darker side: it's not hard to see "keeping up with the Joneses" dynamics in Christian churches. When one family buys a large-screen HDTV or a giant SUV, it's not long before a few others feel compelled to join the club.

Finally, an arrow flows from the middle circle to the inner one, the word of God. At first, we are inclined to say, "Impossible! We cannot change the word of God." That's both true and false. It's true that we cannot change the word of God, but we can and do *interpret* the word of God, and this interpretation may distort the word so that it fits more comfortably with the stories of our culture. For example, the Bible contains ten times as many instructions concerning caring for the poor and avoiding the temptations of wealth than it does about prayer. Yet, many North American Christians are convinced that focusing on prayer is much more central to our walk with God than caring for the poor. Addressing poverty is an uncomfortable and unpopular intrusion in a materialistic culture. In other words, the story of our culture shapes how we read the Bible and thereby can distort our interpretation of the word of God.

One final comment on the three circles: the arrows flowing from the outer to the inner circle are often negative, but not always. For example, historically Christians have not been deeply concerned about the environment, assuming that following God dealt with more "spiritual" matters. During the past thirty years, various voices around the world (many of them non-Christian) have become deeply concerned about the environment, warning that our futures are in deep jeopardy if we continue on this path. Because of these voices, many Christians have discovered that the Bible reveals God's deep concern for his whole creation; everything that is created is a creature of the Lord and is worthy of appropriate respect and care. We can see how the two inward-pointing arrows have worked: voices in the culture have alerted Christians to the issue, and Christians in turn have discovered that the Bible indeed shares this concern.

Table: How the "Circles and Arrows" Operate

	Description	Moving outward	Moving inward
Inner circle	God's Word and Spirit bringing transformation	Word and Spirit draw people to Christ and begin his transforming work	----
Middle circle	The Christian community, being transformed by the Spirit but also affecting each other sinfully	Christians seek to be a salt and a light in their cultural context	Christians interpret God's Word and cooperate with his Spirit in culturally shaped ways
Outer circle	The particular culture in which Christians live	---	Cultural forces shape Christians in many different ways

The Spirit's Transforming Work: Getting Specific

As soon as we aim to understand the nitty-gritty of sanctification and transformation more clearly, we run into a problem. The Spirit challenges us to die and come to life in Christ in every part of our being, but there is not and never will be an official manual that describes all the "parts" that make up our being. To be human is to be fearfully and wondrously made, a mystery that can't be described in formulas or manuals.

Once while I was hitchhiking home from college (from Iowa to southern Ontario), I was picked up by an older man driving from Chicago to Detroit. I remember little of our four-hour conversation, except that at one point he said, "I been married to my woman for forty years, and every time I think I got her figured out, she goes out and does somethin' that surprises me." And then he laughed, as if to say, "And that's the way it's supposed to be." And so it is: we are wondrous mysteries that can't be fit into neat little boxes or programmed by a computer. The whole of our identity is always much greater and deeper than the sum of its parts. We do know that every part of our being is redeemed by the blood of the Lamb and is called to die and to come to new life. Each dimension of our humanity is being sanctified inside the power of God's grace. With that perspective in mind, we'll examine a few of these dimensions, with the purpose of catching a glimpse of the Spirit's work of sanctification.

One more thing to remember: all of these delightfully varied aspects of our humanness are joined together in the human heart, which is in many ways hidden from view. As the Spirit works within each dimension, it also works within our hearts, challenging us to trust in God more fully, exposing our idolatries and strengthening our ability to tune in to God's truth. As you explore a few of these dimensions with me, remember that the human heart underlies the whole picture.

1. The body.

Many years ago, while our family was spending a week at a lakeside cabin, I watched our two-year-old playing in the sand. As he dug trenches, running back and forth from the lake with a small pail to fill them with water, a lovely summer breeze blowing through his hair, I remember thinking to myself, "Wow, he has a beautiful body," and I sang with David, "I praise you because [he is] fearfully and wonderfully made" (Psalm 139:14). That hour felt like a glimpse of Eden, and I wanted to echo the Lord's conclusion after seeing all that he had made, "It was very good" (Genesis 1:31).

God created us as bodily beings, and our bodies belong to the "very goodness" of his creation. But both the Christian faith and contemporary culture often treat our bodies as something troublesome, something to be anxious about. Almost everyone raised in a Christian environment has heard phrases like this since middle school: "Your body is a temple of the Holy Spirit. Therefore, you should not smoke, drink alcohol, or have sex before marriage." There's something right about that advice, but if that's all we emphasize, it reduces the body to a source of anxiety and sin. Becoming new in Christ as bodily beings is much richer than these three "nots."

We experience the Spirit's transforming work as we deepen the *enjoyment* experienced through our bodies. Our five senses connect us so richly to this world: with our bodies we can *see* trees blowing wildly in the wind, blizzarding snow hitting our windowpanes or thousands of stars filling the night sky; we can *hear* the wonder of human voices interacting with ours, a flock of geese honking madly as they pelt by in their lopsided V formations, hundreds of singing worshipers surrounding our own voice with a chorus of praise; we can *taste* a gourmet pasta dish, salt spray on our tongue as we walk along an ocean shore, the love of another in a romantic kiss; we can *feel* the textures of tall grasses, refreshing rain on our faces, the playful collision of bodies in spirited games of football or hockey. Our noses connect us to this world, too, as we breathe in the pulsating energy of busy city traffic, the freshness of a quiet spring sunrise, or the nervous sweat of a roomful of students writing a test. The reality of our sensory experience is vastly greater than the few items listed here because our five senses operate simultaneously, continually pulling in rich, multifaceted experiences.

Perhaps it seems silly to you to begin a discussion of the Spirit sanctifying our bodies by describing enjoyment. After all, it's nice to enjoy things, but that doesn't serve any *real* purpose. Enjoyment is like the dessert; what really matters is the meat and potatoes of the main course. Such thoughts come from a spirit of *utilitarianism,* which simply means that things must be *useful* in order to be important. Enjoyment is pleasant but not particularly useful, and therefore it is secondary. Christians have often embraced utilitarian thinking, assuming that we are called to make our lives useful for God; anything that is not useful is frivolous and a waste of time.

But the Bible is not utilitarian. In describing the garden of Eden, it tells us that "the Lord God made all kinds of trees grow out of the ground—trees that were pleasing to the eye and good for food" (Genesis 2:9). We learn that they were *enjoyable to look at* before we are told that they were also useful for providing food! This combination of enjoyment and usefulness resonates with the first question and answer of the Westminster Catechism: "What is the chief end of man? Man's chief end is to glorify God and to enjoy him forever." Enjoying God involves so much—including using our five senses to enjoy the wonders of the world he made and continues to uphold.

As the Spirit's sanctifying work deepens our ability to enjoy all of these sensations, we discover that one of our most challenging tasks is learning to enjoy our own bodies. Our culture encourages us to experience great discontent with our own bodies; perfect bodily ideals are presented in the media, and a variety of products and activities are marketed with the promise that they will help us approach these ideals. Everywhere we turn there are billboards, magazine covers, and TV commercials proclaiming: "This is the ideal weight for you!" "Here is what your teeth should look like!" "Let us show you the perfect hair color and style." "We can provide the quickest way to achieve a bigger bust, a slimmer waist, more muscular biceps, more hair on your chest." Besides promoting discontent with our own bodies, these messages also encourage us to evaluate the bodies of others according to the ideal. They try to convince us that the shape and look of our body is a central defining feature of our identity and our worth. When they succeed, we become anxious about something that God intended us to enjoy.

Jesus addresses this anxiety, declaring, "I tell you, do not worry about your life, what you will eat or drink; or about your body, what you will wear. Is not life more important than food, and the body more important than clothes? . . . Seek first the kingdom," he advises, "and all these other things will be given to you as well" (Matthew 6:25, 33). The sanctification of our bodies includes honoring the rightful place of the body in our lives, a place that receives every body of every shape, size, and color as a delightful gift from God. Like most matters of sanctification, this is easy to say but very difficult to do. Whenever I walk past a mirror, the voices begin whispering in my ear with their "I wish my body . . ." lists. Silencing those voices and resting in the love of God, through which I am "fearfully and wonderfully made," is hard, lifelong work.

Bodily sanctification continues by respecting our creatureliness. When the gospel declares, "For God so loved the world" (John 3:16), it is telling us that God loves and cares for creatures like us, and part of receiving his love is caring for the bodies that he loves, too. Bodies require sleep, healthy food, invigorating exercise, playful activity. It's good for our bodies to rub shoulders with others, greet others with a firm handshake or a warm bear hug, and encourage one another with a shoulder rub or neck massage. Though our cultural infatuation with slimness is rooted in godless idolatry, the current epidemic of obesity in America is equally disrespectful of the good Lord's care for human bodily life.

Furthermore, physical health is inseparable from our emotional, intellectual, and spiritual health. We are whole creatures, and every part of us is intertwined with every other part. I remember many years ago visiting my pastor in the hospital after he had undergone surgery. After we had chatted for some time, he asked, "Could you pray for me?" I was shocked. He was the man who prayed countless times with people one on one and for our entire congregation during Sunday worship. Why did he ask me to pray for him? When he noticed that I hadn't responded to his request, he continued, "I find it hard to pray in my current condition and need you to say the words on my behalf." So I did. Now I understand his request more clearly: there is a deep connection between physical well-being, spiritual well-being, and every other kind of well-being. Since then, I've had many encounters with folks enduring other kinds of struggles—emotional, relational, intellectual—who requested prayer for similar reasons.

The sanctification of our bodies is greatly helped by the adoption of truth-walking habits and the putting to death of life-denying habits. Many Christians practice Sabbath-rest habits—during part of the day and/or on Sundays—that deepen their enjoyment of God's good creation. Are there habits that can help us enjoy our own bodies? I'm not a great athlete, but for many years, I've played racquetball twice a week, and this habit has been good for my body while strengthening friendships. And whenever I pass a mirror and those slippery voices begin to whisper their taunts about the inadequacies of my body, I've learned to say to them, "Shut up! I will listen to the Lord and not to you!" It may be one of the stranger habits that I practice, but I will continue to do it because I need it. It helps me walk in the truth just a bit more steadily.

Toward the end of his life, the apostle Paul declared, "I eagerly expect and hope that I . . . will have sufficient courage so that now as always Christ will be exalted in my body" (Philippians 1:20). That's a great theme verse to encourage us as the Lord walks with us on the way of sanctifying our bodies.

2. *Emotions.*

Go through a mental checklist: during the last twenty-four hours, how often have you been happy, sad, angry, anxious, numb, eager, afraid, surprised, relieved, and/or disgusted? What has brought on these emotions? Did you "decide" to have them, or did they "just happen"? Do you have any control over them? Have you ever noticed conflicting emotions beating inside you at the same time? Athletes preparing for "the big game" are often eager, excited, and nervous at the same time. Parents watching their son or daughter publicly declare marriage vows share in the deep joy of the day but also feel twinges of sorrow that their child is now definitely leaving their home.

Emotions have a checkered place in human history, celebrated at times and vilified at others. Ecstatic worship and powerful works of art have given testimony to the strength and depth of human emotion; various philosophies and religious beliefs have taught that the emotions are not to be trusted because they are irrational, easily swayed, unstable, and weak. Christian thought also reflects this ambiguity—both extremes can be found, occasionally even within the same person. I find that in the course of one day I can get very frustrated with myself when my emotions put me on an out-of-control roller coaster, yet I can also enjoy the rich colors provided by varied emotions.

This ambiguity becomes exacerbated because our cultural context tends to ascribe too much weight to human emotion. "If it feels right, do it," goes a modern proverb, and truth is what feels right to me. Most Christians reject such blanket celebrations of human feeling, but these tendencies have a significant impact upon us in other ways. "I don't know what's wrong with me," a student once said to me, "God feels so far away right now." A common tendency among us as Christians is to evaluate the quality of our faith life by how close we *feel* to God. When we feel very connected to God, we also feel good about our faith; when God feels far away, we wonder what we're doing wrong. Another time, I asked a high school student on a Monday morning how his weekend had been. "Just great," he smiled, "my girlfriend and I were part of a spiritual retreat, and she got converted again!" I later learned that it was her third "conversion," and I wondered if she had confused "feeling close to God again" with the commitment to surrender her life to him.

Our heart—the "organ" of trust and commitment—is not the same as our emotions. It's difficult to experience this distinction because our trusting and our making commitments have emotions wrapped up inside them. But honoring this distinction is very important in the Christian life. We easily give our emotions the central place that belongs to the heart and substitute feeling close to God for trusting and loving him. I find the Psalms very helpful for understanding this distinction. For example, the writer of Psalm 42 *feels* very discouraged and far from God; he cries out, "I say to God my Rock, 'why have you forgotten me? Why must I go about mourning, oppressed by the enemy?'" (Psalm 42:9) Yet he concludes by telling himself, "Put your hope in God, for I will yet praise him, my Savior and my God" (Psalm 42:11). When things go well, trust is layered over with wonderful feelings, but for those Psalm 42 times when the feelings won't come, trust involves a decision, a heart commitment to place one's hope and trust in God even when feelings seem to mock that decision. It's like a marriage. There are days when I don't *feel* like loving my wife, and those are the days when I must remember the vows that I made and *be a loving husband* regardless of my feelings. Similarly, those times when I feel very far from God are often the exact times when I must remember that he is close to me in spite of my feelings (just read Psalm 139), and I can continue living out of the commitment I made to him. The sanctification of our emotions begins by recognizing that our emotions, while an important part of who we are, cannot replace the central role of our heart.

When emotions occupy the central place in our being, life really does take on a roller-coaster feel. Emotions are very fickle, jerked around by almost anything. In a typical day, they are affected by how well we sleep, the weather, what we eat, whether someone smiles or frowns at us, and a host of such little details. If the center of our faith life can be tossed and turned by such things, we will be unstable people indeed. Every youth leader knows that creating an environment at a weekend retreat or convention in which large groups of teenagers get a "spiritual high" is really quite easy to do. Here's the recipe: take one big-name speaker who knows how to tell just the right stories with dramatic intensity, add in one top-notch worship band and one popular performing band (preferably with a cute drummer), mix in hundreds of teens meeting each other for the first time while living on pop, sugar, and not much sleep, and spiritual highs will arrive in abundance. Even though such experiences can be created through a fairly simple recipe, they can be helpful as long as we remember that faith is not rooted in our emotions.

If our emotions are not at the center of our faith life, where do they belong? We need to begin by acknowledging that emotions are a wondrous dimension of our createdness; they add a profound God-given depth to our lives, enabling us to experience awe, rejoicing, adoration, contentment, and peace. Negative emotions, such as sadness, anger, and discouragement, also point to the depths of our creatureliness; if we experience a tragedy in our lives but are unable to feel sad, we miss something crucial! Some Christians believe that sanctifying our emotions means repressing all negative emotions so that we feel only joy and awe. Fortunately, the Bible has no room whatsoever for this kind of thinking. In the Psalms, that great biblical songbook, we find more laments (songs of sadness, confusion, and anger) than any other kind of song. The Psalmists (those Old Testament worship leaders) knew well that true worship is not emotion-driven but does require *emotional honesty*. Because life in a sinful world includes a great deal to be sad, confused, and angry about, our worship must honor those emotions and bring them to expression. The Christian faith is centered on a relationship between God and his creatures, and a relationship that does not allow one party to be honest with the other will always remain a superficial relationship.

The sanctification of our emotions involves distinguishing our emotions from our trusting heart and being freed for emotional honesty before the face of God. Are there more dimensions to the sanctifying of our emotional life? Surely we cannot *change* our emotions; emotions just happen, we say. A friend frowns at me in the morning and I feel down for the next three hours, wondering if I did something wrong or if she just had a headache; I might feel silly that such a little event affects me so much, but I can't help it. Emotions just happen!

They do—and they don't—just happen. We have very little control over the feelings that arise within us, but we have a great deal of control over how we express those feelings. A young child may throw a temper tantrum whenever he doesn't get his way; that child usually doesn't decide to throw a tantrum, it "just comes." A patient parent (an oxymoron?) will very gradually seek to teach that child that a temper tantrum is not an appropriate way to respond and will coach the child in learning more constructive ways of dealing with disappointment. Most children eventually catch on.

The same is true for the whole of our emotional life: very gradually we grow toward emotional maturity. For example, the Bible describes one aspect of Christian community as "rejoicing with those who rejoice and weeping with those who weep" (Romans 12:15). Many of us are naturally nervous about weeping with the sorrowing, and we'd rather ignore them or make some pseudospiritual comment such as, "Don't worry, God will work things out for the best." But we can *learn* to weep with the sorrowing; we can grow toward an emotional maturity that is able to be genuinely sad with a fellow brother or sister. If we find ourselves anxiously wanting to ignore another's sorrow, we can give such nervousness to the Holy Spirit and pray, "Lord, this situation scares me but I know that I am called to share in this person's sadness. Help me to take baby steps in that direction." That is a prayer for the sanctification of our emotions.

Because our emotions are so mysterious, their sanctification requires great patience, and shortcuts usually do more harm than good. For example, I once heard someone say, "Anger is a dangerous emotion that usually leads to sin; I have resolved that I will never be angry." The Bible never says that anger is always sinful. In his famous love chapter, Paul tells us that "love is not *easily* angered" (1 Corinthians 13:5, emphasis mine). He advises the Ephesians, "In your anger do not sin. Do not let the sun go down while you are still angry, and do not give the devil a foothold" (Ephesians 4:26–27). These two teachings tell us that anger is something that requires proper care, but it should not be abolished. There is a time when love requires anger, but not anger that arises easily. When we are angry, we must process it, work it through, come to some kind of resolution as quickly as we can (before the sun goes down!). And when we do not deal with anger in a healthy way, we are providing room for the devil to do significant damage. One way in which our emotions are sanctified comes through dealing with anger properly, but that is just one example. Each one of our emotions is gradually refined in a fire as the Holy Spirit continues to work on us.

3. The mind or intellect.

I'll never forget a conversation I had with sixteen-year-old Jesse about his faith. He loved the Lord and was eager to become a more mature Christian. I suggested some ways in which he could learn to think more deeply about the teachings of the Christian faith. He was silent for a time and looked at me with skepticism in his eyes. Finally he said, "As you know, my older brother Rob has been studying at the university the last two years. You also know that Rob is a deep thinker who wants to examine every side of a question before coming to any conclusions. Every time I talk to Rob, it seems like his faith is shakier than it was the time before, and I'm sure that all of his deep thought is just messing with his faith. I don't think I should make the same mistake. I don't think it's good for me to think more deeply about the Christian faith."

Jesse's experience with his brother Rob reflects a centuries-old conundrum: what is the role of our intellect in our walk with God? Is it a help or a hindrance? Is it wisest to follow Rob's example or Jesse's example, or do we need to find a third way? In other words, what is involved with God's sanctifying work as it is applied to our intellect?

Like emotions, the intellect has occupied a confused place in the history of the Christian faith. And, also like our emotions,

two extremes can be found. On the one hand, the mind is sometimes given such a central place that it takes over what rightly
belongs to the heart. The Christian faith then becomes primarily
about *right understanding,* which involves an intellectual account
of God, of doctrine, and of Scripture. Growing in faith is reduced to obtaining more "correct knowledge," and Christians
evaluate the integrity of each other's faith according to how correct and complete their knowledge is. Christian worship may
focus primarily around a lecturelike sermon, with "warm-up"
and "wind down" activities that lead up to and flow from the
sermon. The sermon is a good one if it delivers solid intellectual
content and deepens my knowledge of God. One of the most
important goals of the Christian life is to ensure that I have my
doctrine right; if mine is right but yours is not, then we cannot
belong to the same denomination. One of us will have to leave
and join another one or start a new one. The fact that today
there are many thousands of Christian denominations, and, especially more recently, thousands of independent, nondenomi-
national congregations, often illustrates either (a) giving the
intellect a central place in Christian faith life, or (b) reacting
against giving the intellect a central place.

The latter extreme—reacting against the intellect—is also very
common today. Emotion-driven emphases are partnered with a
view that faith life does not require solid, intellectual doctrinal
thinking. After all, such thinking only serves to divide the church
and tends to focus on minor matters instead of what really counts.
"The main thing is to keep the main thing the main thing," and the
"main thing" is not doctrine or intellectual thought; it's trusting
in Jesus. That's true, but is it really an either/or issue? Do we
either trust or think? Recently, a friend said to me, "I think one
of our most dangerous hymns is 'Trust and Obey' because too
many Christians assume that trusting is a nonthinking activity."
Similarly, I heard a preacher begin a sermon on Romans 12 by

saying, "Too many Christians that I know change one word in Paul's instructions so that he says "Do not conform any longer to the pattern of this world, but be transformed by the removing [instead of "renewing"] of your mind" (Romans 12:2). Like Jesse, many Christians are afraid to think.

But the apostle Paul had no such fear. The Romans 12:2 quote leads to the question "What is involved in the renewing—in the sanctification—of our mind or intellect?" First of all, as with human emotion, our intellect must not occupy the center of our faith life, but it is an important dimension of our walk with God. Its sanctification involves honoring its rightful place. God created us as intellectual beings, capable of analyzing and understanding a great deal. We are called to love him with all of our "heart, soul, strength, and *mind.*" How do we love him with our minds? The love of a trusting heart is encouraged, stretched, and deepened by the love of a searching, analyzing, wisdom-seeking mind.

Remembering how God reveals himself to us in the Bible and in creation guides us in sanctifying the intellect. The Bible is not a scientific textbook that we are called to memorize so that we can answer multiple-choice questions on a final exam (judgment day). Neither is it a praise chorus that repeats "Our God is an awesome God" over and over again. Rather, the Bible tells the story of God's faithfulness to his creation and of his creatures responding to him, and this story is the story of our own lives. Reading the Bible *begins* by receiving it as God's love letter to us. Have you ever received a love letter? The first response is a *relational* one; I have received a communication that deeply connects me to the communicator! We are bound together somehow. The Bible serves to deepen my love, trust, praise, and adoration for its author.

But the Bible is vastly different from any love letter that I have ever received. It has 1,189 chapters written by more than

100 authors over a period longer than 1,500 years! Its writings are very complex—theologically, ethically, culturally, and literarily. Even with all of the combined intellectual resources available to me, my community, and the church of the ages, I cannot understand everything written in this love letter. Even so, I am called to try to understand it as well as it can be understood. Therefore, my intellect is a crucial vehicle for deepening my love and trust in God. God dared to write us such a complex and difficult book because he created us with an intellect; using that intellect well is one way of loving him.

But there is much more! God also shows himself to us in his creation, and this piece of his revelation is even more varied, complex, and difficult to understand. Every major offered at college focuses on developing an intellectual understanding of one tiny corner (one square inch) of God's creation. Just as the Bible nourishes my love and trust for God while also challenging me intellectually, so the study of psychology nourishes my sense of the wonder and mystery of God's creation of humankind and my sense of sorrow for the brokenness so evident within human creatures. The study of history reveals the complexities of human motivation, political and economic maneuvering, the interweaving of sin and grace on an international scale. Every farmer knows that the field of agriculture has become troublingly complex with advances in biotechnology and economic forces that imperil the traditional family farmstead. Sanctifying the intellect begins by honoring God the creator who formed us with minds capable of hard, analytic work and continues by honoring the depths of his revelation in Scripture and creation by our rejecting simplistic answers and probing the mysteries of his wonder-filled world. One of our deepest callings during our college years is to become stronger lovers of God with *all* of our mind, strengthening a foundation that encourages us on our way as lifelong lovers.

The biblical term that best captures the sanctification of the intellect is *wisdom*. Wisdom integrates rigorous intellectual understanding, common sense, and relational skills that know how to say the right words at the right time in the right tone of voice. Wisdom understands the difference between what is knowable and what must remain a mystery to humankind. An old saying states, "It's possible to get straight As and flunk life," reminding us that "being smart" is very different from "being wise." Growing in wisdom is central to deepening the colors of life before the face of God because "wisdom is more precious than rubies, and nothing you desire can compare with her" (Proverbs 8:11). The next chapter will explore the seeking of wisdom in more detail.

4. Desires.

A young mother announced to her family that she was heading out to the mall to pick up a few things. Immediately, four-year-old Angela dropped her toys and came running, calling out, "Mommy, can I come, can I come?" Her mom looked at her hesitantly and asked, "Do you remember what happened the last time you came?" Angela's chin sagged to her chest, her lower lip curled out, and she nodded without saying a word. Her mom smiled and said, "You can come if you promise to leave your 'I wants' at home. Do you promise?" Angela nodded again, more cheerfully this time.

Have you ever tried to leave your "I wants" at home? It's not that easy. Angela's mom knew that her daughter could not actually leave them at home, but Angela had promised that she would not whine or nag about things she wanted her mom to buy. Her wants would still be there, but they would be silent.

Our wants are always there. The Lord created us as desiring creatures. An important dimension of our humanness is that we are conscious of time: we are creatures who remember the past and anticipate the future as we live in the present. Anticipation produces desire: we desire certain realities to become part of our future, and then we work (in the present) toward realizing these desires. It's astounding how much of our life is actually caught up seeking to obtain a desire of some kind. College study has an element of preparing for a career; a friendship may grow into a marriage; as I write this page, I desire to see a finished product. We are goal-directed people, involved in many activities that—we hope—will lead to desired outcomes. Try making a list of every desire that is woven inside your life during a twenty-four-hour period; the list would be very long.

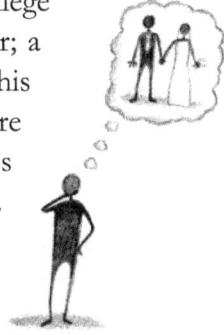

God created us with desire, and his creation was very good, so our desiring was part of that goodness. Sin infected our desiring, too, and now God's redeeming/sanctifying work transforms our desires toward the goodness it once knew. The Bible teaches that all of our desires are called to fit under one foundational desire: the desire to see God's kingdom come. This foundational desire embraces a host of other desires. My desires to complete college, be a good friend, stay healthy, fight injustice, encourage a struggling classmate, be married someday, enjoy God's creation, or relax after finishing some hard work can all feed into the central desire to seek first the kingdom of God. Jesus describes the connection between the "many" desires and the "central" desire this way: "Do not worry, saying, 'What shall we eat?' or 'What shall we drink?' or 'What shall we wear?' For the pagans run after all these things, and your heavenly Father knows that you need them. But seek first his kingdom and his righteousness, and all these things will be added to you as well" (Matthew 6:31–33). This echoes a beatitude from the previous chapter, "Blessed are those who hunger and thirst for righteousness, for they will be filled" (Matthew 5:6). "Seeking," "hungering" and "thirsting" are all synonyms for "desiring."

The Holy Spirit sanctifies our desires by collecting our "many" desires and placing them under the umbrella of desiring the kingdom and righteousness.

But many of our desires do not fit with the coming of the kingdom. What can I do about that? Desires just "happen"; can I actually control them? They come up in my consciousness without any effort on my part. I have desires that are not very wholesome, I don't like them, and I often feel powerless in getting rid of them. Does the Holy Spirit actually sanctify my desires?

Jesus's teachings in Matthew 5–6 would be utterly foolish if our desires were "nonsanctifiable." Remember two important details about sanctification: it usually happens very gradually, and no part of it is finished during our lifetimes. Though we will struggle with unwholesome desires for our entire lives, our desires can truly be transformed by the Holy Spirit. I have talked with seventh graders who were convinced that they would die if they could not wear $150 running shoes to school, and three years later they realized how silly that desire had been. A psalmist promises, "Delight yourself in the Lord and he will give you the desires of your heart" (Psalm 37:4). This promise is not suggesting that delighting in the Lord results in every desire of ours being fulfilled by the Lord. Rather, it promises that delighting in him leads to the *growth* of godly desires and the *dying* of desires that do not fit with delighting in the Lord. In other words, the Psalm promises the sanctification of our desires.

I frequently hear students say something like, "I would love to serve the Lord as a computer technician, but I'm not sure if this desire is from the Lord or if it's just something *I want* to do." It's a good thing to wonder about our desires, but putting it this way often isn't helpful. Godly desires often are *both* from the Lord *and* something that I want to do. Christians assume at times that if I want something, it must come from selfish desires and not from the Lord. But if (as the Psalm promises) God gives us the desires of our heart, then godly desires more and more become that which we ourselves want to do.

God sanctifies our desires in two ways. First, desires that have no place inside the kingdom are called to die. I remember speaking with a young man whose wife had just left him. He said, "After finishing school and entering the workforce, all I wanted to do was buy the biggest and best of everything that I could: cars, entertainment centers, weekend trips, I wanted it all. My parents just shook their heads as they continued living a more sensible, simple life. Now my life has fallen apart, and I can see that I was running down a dead-end street." Thankfully, we don't usually need to have our lives fall apart to put ungodly desires to death. As we mature in Christ, we recognize that certain things that once seemed absolutely essential to our well-being are actually unnecessary and quite possible hurtful, like those $150 running shoes.

Second, God sanctifies our desires by realigning them so that they fit more closely with the coming of his kingdom. Sin-driven desires can be transformed into kingdom-seeking desires. For example, I may desire to become a lawyer because I imagine that I'll earn a huge income, achieve a high social status, and impress my parents. Eventually I may see the emptiness of my reasoning and desire to become a lawyer because I have a passion for justice and I recognize how easy it is for life to push the needy down in terribly unfair ways. My original desire was driven more by idolatry than my love for the Lord. My desire to become a lawyer survived, but the "drive" inside the desire was transformed. When I put my own desires under a microscope, I discover that almost all of them are a mixture of Holy Spirit "stuff" and "other stuff," because I listen to two or three different "radio stations" at the same time. As I give my desires to the Lord to be sanctified, I pray that he will strengthen the leading of the Spirit and put to death that other stuff.

When you feel discouraged about the sanctification of your desires, remember that God's best work is usually very slow and gradual. Some years ago, the oldest member of our congregation died at the age of ninety-seven. One of the elders at the church recounted the story of visiting her and her husband when they were "youngsters" in their midseventies and reading Colossians 3 with them. He said, "I was a young and nervous elder, and as I read to them 'put to death sexual immorality, impurity, lust . . .' (v. 5), I stopped reading and said, 'Sorry, I know this doesn't really apply to you.'" As he continued reading, he noticed that the woman was quietly giggling in the background. He turned red in the face, finished the passage, and asked, "Why are you giggling?" She replied, "Young man, that's a beautiful passage, but your comment shows that you don't understand older folks very well yet." The Lord hadn't finished sanctifying her sexual desires yet; she needed to hear that verse, too.

5. Dreams.

Every day, we live with dozens of different types of desires, but some of our desires are in a special category of their own: our desires on the grandest scale possible are our dreams for the future.

Have you ever watched young children play make-believe games? Have you seen them play house or school or pretend to be NASCAR champions? Why do children all over the world need to imagine themselves in adult situations?

Young children's make-believe games are not simply meaningless play. Such games illustrate one of the most important dimensions of our creation: we are created to imagine the future. We are made to dream dreams and place ourselves inside those dreams.

Dreaming doesn't stop when we leave childhood behind. What dreams do you have for yourself as you imagine life ten or twenty years from now? How have these dreams changed since you were a young child or a high school student?

Dreams are important because God created us not only as creatures who are able to *imagine* a future; we are also able to *take steps* toward the future that we have imagined. Our dreams for the future play a major role in *how we live now* because dreams motivate our actions. We were created to form dreams and then seek to realize these dreams.

How do our dreams for the future intersect with God's work of sanctification? In three principal ways. First, God is leading this world to the future that he has prepared for it, and he gives us the Holy Spirit to grow dreams in us that are in line with his future. We don't often associate the Holy Spirit with our dreams for the future, but that association is one of the first things mentioned about the Spirit on Pentecost Sunday. When the Spirit is poured out on Pentecost, the watching crowd in Jerusalem thinks that the Spirit-filled disciples are drunk. Peter declares to them,

> These men are not drunk as you suppose. It's only nine in the morning! No, this is what was spoken by the prophet Joel: "In the last days, God says, I will pour out my Spirit on all people. Your sons and daughters will prophesy, your young men will see visions and your old men will dream dreams." (Acts 2:15–17)

Peter points out that one of the results of the Holy Spirit living in us is that we grow godly dreams, and we do so because the Holy Spirit is "a deposit, guaranteeing what is to come" (2 Corinthians 1:22). In other words, God is making everything new, and the Holy Spirit is like a down payment, a small beginning, of that newness, leading us to dream dreams describing what the newness will be like and then take steps toward that newness.

The Bible gives us many examples of such dreams to help guide our own Holy Spirit dreams. Listen to just a few of them:

Every warrior's boot used in battle and every garment rolled in blood will be destined for burning, will be fuel for the fire. (Isaiah 9:5)

The wolf will live with the lamb, the leopard will lie down with the goat, the calf and the lion and the yearling together, and a little child will lead them. (Isaiah 11:6)

You will go out in joy and be led forth in peace; the mountains and the hills will burst into song before you, and all the trees of the field will clap their hands. (Isaiah 55:12)

Is not this the kind of fasting I have chosen: to loose the chains of injustice and untie the cords of the yoke, to set the oppressed free and break every yoke? Is it not to share food with the hungry and to provide the poor wanderer with shelter—when you see the naked to clothe him, and not to turn away from your own flesh and blood? Then your light will break forth like the dawn, and your healing will quickly appear; then your righteousness will go before you, and the glory of the Lord will be your rear guard. (Isaiah 58: 6–8)

I pray that out of his [the Father's] glorious riches he may strengthen you with power through His spirit in your inner being, so that Christ may dwell in your hearts through faith. And I pray that you, being rooted and established in love, may have power, together with all the saints, to grasp how wide and long and high and deep is the love of Christ, and to know this love that surpasses knowledge—that you may be filled to the measure of all the fullness of God. (Ephesians 3:16–19)

Speaking the truth in love, we will in all things grow up into him who is the Head, that is Christ. From him the whole body, joined and held together by every supporting ligament, grows and builds itself up in love, as each part does its work. (Ephesians 4:15–16)

Then I saw a new heaven and a new earth, for the first heaven and the first earth had passed away. . . . And I heard a loud voice from the throne saying, "Now the dwelling of God is with men, and he will live with them. . . . There will be no more death or mourning or crying or pain, for the old order of things has passed away." (Revelation 21:1–4)

Combine verses like these with many more such descriptions in the Bible and a picture of shalom emerges. We are called to dream "shalomful" dreams and live toward these dreams. The Holy Spirit is a down payment of these dreams, enabling us to begin to walk inside these dreams now.

Second, Holy Spirit dream formation occurs in competition with *cultural* dream formation. In the mid-1990s, millions of middle school boys dreamed of becoming the next Michael Jordan. A few years ago, an investment company ran television ads for a product they called "Freedom Fifty-Five." They showed clips of couples in their midfifties snorkeling in Hawaii, yachting in the Caribbean, and playing golf in the Carolinas. As these appealing images rolled by, the narrator promised, "invest with us and you can retire at fifty-five and do all of these things." The advertising industry knows that our dreams are shaped by our deepest values, and human beings have an innate craving for freedom and pleasure.

In North America, the common dreams of the culture involve finding fulfilling careers, owning a decent home with two cars, and enjoying colorful vacation trips. Having families with many (five or more) children doesn't fit very well with these dreams, so during the past forty years the average number of children per family has dropped considerably. Friends of ours left their comfortable middle-class lifestyle and moved with their three children to rural Indonesia and worked there for four years as agricultural consultants. They were deeply struck by one farmer who looked at them pityingly and said, "you are poor; you have only three children." With his seven children, he had fulfilled a dream of his culture: large families that provide more helping hands to generate more income. Societies have ways of loudly declaring, "this is what matters, shape your dreams accordingly," and these declarations come to seem so *normal* that assessing how Holy Spirit–inspired dreams might look different becomes very difficult. Therefore, a crucial part of the sanctification of our dreams involves recognizing the ways in which our dreams have been shaped by the dreams of our culture and contrasting this shaping with biblically based, Holy Spirit–inspired dreams.

Finally, our dreams are formed by the way in which our past experiences have stimulated our imagination. In other words, to quite an extent the options that we can picture for our future are shaped by the ways we have experienced life in our past. A former student of mine, Justin, loved playing football in high school and developed a very close relationship with his coach. Because of an injury, he received weekly physical therapy for a time and was very impressed by the ways in which Jerry, the therapist, worked over his shoulder. Justin enjoyed studying the sciences, and so a dream began to grow inside him of becoming a physical therapist himself.

During his first semester in college he took several science courses and volunteered as an assistant football coach at a local high school. By Christmas, he realized three things connected to his dream: (1) he loved working with the local football team; (2) the science courses were not stimulating his passion the way he had expected; and (3) the course he enjoyed the most was his required first-year history course. By January, his dream had been revised, and Justin imagined himself as a high school history and physical education teacher. The new experiences of college had reshaped his imagination and his dream formation.

Our experiences concerning what it means to be male or female also affect the shaping of our dreams. Every culture on earth conveys particular assumptions concerning what it means to be a man or a woman and what sorts of dreams are acceptable for each gender. For example, North American culture cultivates dreams of the "career woman," and, in reaction to that, various Christian subcultures have encouraged dreams of the "stay-at-home mom." The Bible does neither. When it dreams about the "wife of noble character," it describes her as someone who "considers a field and buys it, out of her earnings she plants a vineyard. She sets about her work vigorously; her arms are strong for her tasks. She sees that her trading is profitable, and her lamp does not go out at night. . . . She opens her arms to the poor and extends her hands to the needy" (Proverbs 31:16–18, 20). In other words, such a woman is very active in all parts of society.

We are called to dream dreams—dreams inspired by the Holy Spirit on the way to God's future, dreams that are not "conformed to the pattern of this world" but "are transformed by the renewing of our mind" (Romans 12:2); dreams that are stimulated by the broadest range of life experiences and teaching that we can find. We can see these dynamics of dream formation in this conversation between a college student and an elderly monk:

> One day a monk was talking to an energetic young man named Robert. The monk asked what plans he had for the future.
>
> "I want to earn a Law degree as soon as possible," the young man replied.
>
> "And then?" the monk asked.
>
> "Well, then I would like to set up a law firm, then marry and have a family."
>
> "And then, Robert?"
>
> "To be honest," the young man continued, "I would like to earn a lot of money, retire as soon as possible and travel all over the world. I have always wanted to do that."
>
> "And then?" The monk continued almost rudely.
>
> "I have no further plans for the moment," Robert replied.
>
> The monk looked at him and said, "Your plans are too limited. They reach only eighty years into the future. Your plans should be broad enough to include God and all eternity."[‡]

[‡] Barry, Norris, Yeo et al, *Wisdom from the Monastery* (Liturgical Press, 2006) p. 120.

6. Character.

The preacher Charles Swindoll writes, "Character is who you are when nobody is looking." His definition helps me realize how easily "who I am" is shaped by "whom I am with." The greater the differences between "who I am when I am with others" and "who I am when I am alone," the more my character is called into question. I once heard another preacher say, "Integrity means that your inside matches your outside." God's sanctifying work on my character focuses especially on my integrity. Integrity closes the gap between my inside and my outside, between the me "alone" and the me "with others."

Sometimes we confuse *character* with *personality.* They are actually very different. *Personality* focuses on my uniquenesses: I am shy, you are outgoing; I am more emotional, you are more intellectual; I learn best through verbal communication, you learn best when you can visualize something. *Character* involves those qualities that come to expression through our uniquenesses. My character tells you how dependable, honest, loving, and wise I may be. God created us with delightful differences, just as he created thousands of different flowers, birds, insects, and colors. As he sanctifies our character, our unique personalities become more obvious. Weak character tries to fit in with others and minimize uniquenesses; mature character is at peace with itself and enjoys celebrating its uniqueness. Some folks think that Christianity tries to turn all its adherents into clones of one another, but in fact the opposite is true. As C. S. Lewis says, "The more we get what we now call 'ourselves' out of the way and let Him take us over, the more truly ourselves we become. . . . It is when I turn to Christ, when I give myself up to His Personality, that I first begin to have a real personality of my own" (*Mere Christianity,* 174). Being-sanctified character is more free to express its own personality.

God's maturing of my character is growing a kind of *sturdiness* in me that can be compared to a tree growing strong and vibrant. I have written hundreds of reference letters for my students over the years, and in each letter, I describe something of the student's character. My letters tend to look something like this: "Leah's character is shaped very much by integrity. I am impressed by her dependability; she does what she says she will do. She is self-disciplined, able to set her priorities well and live according to the priorities she has set. She has the humble heart of a servant, eager to learn from others and eager to make a contribution wherever she can. She does find it difficult to be honest about her frustrations, but she is aware of that difficulty and I am impressed by the progress she has made in working on that area." Imagine that someone who knows you well would write a character reference on your behalf. What would that paragraph look like?

7. Relationships.

The first six dimensions we have considered deal with realities that happen "inside" us individually (though they are affected very much by other people). My body, emotions, intellect, desires, and character all have to do with *me* as a separate person. Of course, my sense of how others treat my body, react to my emotions, engage my intellect, and so on has a deep effect on me, but each of these realities are personal realities.

One of the first things that God said about us was that "it is not good for the man to be alone" (Genesis 2:18). We are deeply relational, and the Bible from beginning to end describes us as interpersonal creatures. In his famous meditation/poem, John Donne writes, "No man is an island, entire of itself/every man is a piece of the continent, a part of the main." When I hear of prisoners who spend their entire lives in solitary confinement, seeing only the hand of a guard pass a tray of food through a slot three times a day, I shudder inside. We need people, we need relationships.

Relationships also benefit from the Holy Spirit's sanctifying work in our lives. The Bible's insistence that we forgive one another is the centerpiece of relational sanctification. We're all sinners, and the more intimate we become with others, the more our sin affects others too. I'm always shocked by how strong the Bible's language about forgiveness is: "If you forgive men when they sin against you, your heavenly Father will also forgive you. But if you do not forgive men their sins, your Father will not forgive your sins" (Matthew 6:14–15). Jesus *almost* sounds as though he is teaching that we must earn the Father's forgiveness by first forgiving others. Instead, he is teaching us that if we truly receive the Father's grace and forgiveness, then we will become *contagious* with that grace and forgiveness by forgiving others. In other words, if we do not forgive others, we have also rejected God's forgiving us. The sanctification of our relationships begins by dying to the grudges we carry against others and by coming to new life in God's grace shaping our relationships.

The college years add significant new stresses to our relationships. I roomed with one of my closest high school friends when I went to college, and that experience almost destroyed our friendship (thankfully, we are still close today, more than three decades later). Many students move in with a total stranger, and what happens then is completely unpredictable and may be very challenging. Our tendency is to let relationships flow on "automatic pilot": we just hang out with people, and whatever happens, happens. In reality, mature relationships require hard work—the hard work of forgiveness, of being honest when something bothers us, of working on a relationship when we would rather go off alone somewhere, of trying to communicate well when misunderstandings arise.

A fictional story shows how this works. Richard and Jon met during their first semester of college, and they got along well. Every evening, they spent two hours together in Jon's dorm room on his Playstation; their skills were about equally matched and they loved the same games. In October, the midterm grades came out; Jon had earned one F, one D and three Cs. He was shocked; he knew that his grades weren't going to shine, but he had thought that he was passing all his courses. Just after Jon had received his grades, he bumped into Richard as both were on their way back to the dorm. Richard noticed that Jon seemed angry and discouraged, and quickly found out why.

As the two continued walking back to the dorm, their friendship was at a "fork-in-the-road relationship sanctification" moment. They had two choices: they could simply continue their friendship as it was and decide that Jon's grades had no implications for their relationship, or they could decide to deepen their friendship and use it to support and encourage Jon in his need to become a stronger student. Even though it was a dramatic moment, the conversation that followed was quite ordinary:

"You know," said Jon, "I think I better lay off PS every night until my homework is done." "Yea, sounds like a good idea," replied Richard, "I won't bug you if you've still got work to do."

"Thanks," said Jon, and he knew that their friendship had just become deeper and more supportive.

What he probably didn't know was that their friendship was being sanctified, reflecting the kind of encouragement God provides more fully, with deeper colors. Most of our relationships hit "fork-in-the-road" moments when they either deepen or our own sanctification requires that they die. Proverbs celebrates this deepening as it declares, "Wounds from a friend can be trusted . . . perfume and incense bring joy to the heart, and the pleasantness of one's friend springs from his earnest counsel" (Proverbs 27:6, 9).

Sometimes, of course, relationships are meant to die; after all, not everyone that we date is meant to be our future spouse and not every friend that we have is intended to be a lifelong friend.

8. Actions.

Most Christians are hit between the eyes at one time or another by these blunt words from the apostle James: "Faith, if it is not accompanied by action, is dead" (James 2:17). Paul expresses the same thought more gently when he writes, "Whatever you do, whether in word or deed, do it all in the name of the Lord Jesus, giving thanks to God the Father through him" (Colossians 3:17). Paul puts it very simply: our actions are what we do and say, and we are all doing *something* 24/7 (even if it is sleeping). Basically, then, the sanctification of our actions is about the cumulative effect of the sanctification that occurs in every part of our lives, our heart, our body, our emotions, our intellect, our character, our relationships, and every other part of our being.

The Bible often compares our sanctification to the growth of a plant or tree, and then describes our actions as the fruit. A godly person "is like a tree planted by streams of water, which yields its fruit in season" (Psalm 1:3). "I am the vine and you are the branches," teaches Jesus. "If a man remains in me and I in him, he will bear much fruit" (John 15:5). Fruit provides visible evidence that invisible Holy Spirit roots of faith are growing. As James writes, "What good is it if a man claims to have faith but has no deeds? Suppose a brother or sister is without clothes and daily food. If one of you says to him, "Go, I wish you well, keep warm and well fed," but does nothing about his physical needs, what good is it?" (James 2:14–16).

There's something paradoxical about the sanctification of our actions: healthy fruit does not self-consciously work hard to be healthy fruit. It's just the natural result when the roots and the rest of the plant are healthy. When an action is performed under a huge banner that declares "this is a kingdom action done in Jesus's name!" it tends to backfire in the following ways. First, this claim suggests that some actions are more "Christian" than others, undermining Paul's exhortation to do *all* in the name of Jesus. Second, the history of the Christian faith reveals that such loud banners tend to be used to judge, overpower, and marginalize others. Jesus's name has been used to justify massacres, forced conversions, racism, and other forms of prejudice. Jesus's parable about the actions of the Christian life—feeding the hungry, clothing the naked, visiting the sick (Matthew 25:31–46)—features Christians serving others who had no idea that they were actually serving Jesus. There was something unself-consciously anonymous about their actions. Just as Paul's verse concerning doing *all* comes at the end of a teaching about dying and rising in Christ, so actions are discussed last here because fruit grows best when other dimensions of our being— including our heart, our desires, our emotions, our intellect—are on the way of sanctification.

A danger in describing sanctification in terms of these eight dimensions addressed here is that daily life is not so neatly compartmentalized. I do my best intellectual work when I am deeply involved emotionally with the material I am studying, when my body is alert and healthy, when my intellect is motivated by desires to grow in learning, and when other people stimulate my interest in the topic. In daily life, all of the dimensions of my being are completely intertwined; describing them here one by one may be helpful for glimpsing the picture of God's sanctifying work in all that I am and do, but this approach does have its limitations.

Furthermore, we have just scratched the surface of who we are in Christ and how his Spirit does its sanctifying work within us. We could also look at our will, our speech, our commitments, and much more. These eight aspects serve to illustrate how every dimension of our identity, of our lives, is under construction, dying and rising, sharing in Christ's death and resurrection.

Group Sanctification

When our oldest child was in third grade, she sat in front of two fourth graders on the school bus. One day at supper, she said to us, "Rebecca and MaryAnn sit behind me on the bus and most days they're mean. But when Rebecca is gone, MaryAnn is nice and when MaryAnn is gone, Rebecca is nice." She couldn't figure out why things worked out that way.

She discovered something on that school bus that we might call the need for "group sanctification." Group sanctification simply means this: when people come together in groups, a certain dynamic sets in, a certain kind of group personality that communicates very clearly how that group walks with God (which is different from the way in which each member of the group walks with God). One can see it in how the group members treat each other, how they treat those outside the group, how they determine who belongs to the group, and how the group's members are valued in relation to one another. Rebecca and MaryAnn were the "group," and our daughter was an "outsider" who experienced the group personality. When one of the fourth graders was gone, the group was also gone, and the dynamics changed radically. Part of the mystery of a group is that the "whole" is not the sum of the "parts." The parts—Rebecca and MaryAnn on their own—were (as our daughter said) "nice," but when they were put together they were "mean." Each of us is being sanctified individually, but the groups that we are part of also are called to sanctification.

Think of all of the groups that have played a significant role in your own faith life. Most of our lists would include the following: family (both our nuclear family and our extended family), home congregation, youth group, and friendship circle. Sometimes our places of employment, sports teams or musical groups, and places where we do volunteer work are also on the list. Each group develops its own personality, and this group personality is called to participate in the sanctifying work of the Holy Spirit.

I remember the first time I served as an elder in my church. I was given the tasks of visiting about fifteen families in the church once a year to encourage them in their walk with the Lord and of attending a monthly council meeting during which the elders discussed and made decisions concerning various matters of church life. The pastor at the time was a very wise man who knew how to lead us so that our group personality was challenged to be sanctified.

I remember one conversation very clearly. The pastor had recently begun his work in our church. We were discussing a proposal to renovate the pulpit area, and one elder reported, "I talked to Henry Blackman [a wealthy businessman] yesterday, and he mentioned that if we renovate the pulpit area he would probably leave the church, because he designed and financed the original pulpit design twenty years ago and is very emotionally attached to it." Our pastor was quiet for a few moments, then replied, "Well, we have to do what is best. If that goes against Henry's wishes, I hope he enjoys his new church."

I'll never forget the atmosphere in the room after we all heard that statement. Several elders had always been afraid of Henry, because he had a way of pushing his power and influence around. But we all knew that the pastor was right, and we all could sense a kind of sturdiness fill the room, as though everyone was thinking, "He's right. We don't operate by intimidation and manipulation here. We operate by wisdom." The group became stronger; the pastor led us to be more in line with the Holy Spirit, to be more open to the Spirit's work of sanctification.

Group sanctification is a hard concept to grasp, because we live in the most individualistic culture that has ever existed on Planet Earth. We think of faith primarily as "my personal relationship with Jesus Christ," and hardly at all as the Spirit working on the groups that we are part of. But if we would identify the ways in which we have matured in our faith over the years, we would probably notice that the bulk of our maturing has occurred because we were part of groups that the Lord was working on: family, church, friends, and so on. Group sanctification is a crucial part of God's way with us.

Most of Scripture was originally addressed to groups, not individuals. Paul begins almost every one of his letters by thanking God for the way in which the group he is writing to is being sanctified. Listen to one of these passages:

> I always thank God for you because of his grace given you in Christ Jesus. For in him you have been enriched in every way—in all your speaking and in all your knowledge—because our testimony about Christ was confirmed in you. Therefore you do not lack any spiritual gift as you eagerly wait for our Lord Jesus Christ to be revealed. (1 Corinthians 1:4–7)

The rest of the letter clearly tells us that there were quite a few individuals in the Corinthian church living in sin, but Paul is able to thank God for his grace growing in the group as a whole.

The reality of group sanctification has three implications for us as we seek to have our colors deepened by the Spirit of God.

First, it helps us to see how important groups are. God works *in* groups and *through* groups. Because sanctification happens so slowly and because groups are such a natural part of our lives that we hardly notice them, it's easy to be blind to God's sanctifying work in them. Imagine for a moment that your walk with God had no "group content," that your family and friends had nothing to do with God, and that you never were part of a church. How different would you be?

Second, as adulthood gives us considerably more choice concerning which groups we belong to, group sanctification impresses upon us how important these choices are. Do I need to belong to a church? Does it matter who my friends are? Is it important how much I keep in touch with my family after I move a thousand miles away from them? Can't I serve the Lord in any workplace? A lawyer once told me, "When I finished law school, I didn't care where I worked. I found a firm in a city that I liked and was excited to start. I soon realized that this firm was completely driven by money, money, money, and my identity as a Christian was slowly but surely being suffocated in that place. I had to find a new place to work." He wasn't saying that Christians can only work for Christian companies; he was saying that every group has a group personality that either furthers or smothers the work of the Holy Spirit.

Third, as we are being sanctified, we are called to foster an openness to the Spirit's work of group sanctification. Just as that wise pastor helped our church council become more sturdy in the Lord, so we are called to find ways to strengthen the Spirit's presence in our groups. Sometimes a particular wing in the dorm may bond together in Christ in particularly vibrant ways; as we look more closely we see that two or three people are providing the leadership that allows this to happen. A group of friends drifts along aimlessly, concerned only about having a good time, and then something changes. We look more closely and discover that one or two of them have experienced a type of "wake-up call" from the Lord, and they challenge the entire group to take their faith more seriously.

Every fall, I meet new classes of students, and one of my tasks is to facilitate the sanctification of the classroom. My goal is to grow a classroom in which students care deeply about what they are learning, respect each other's viewpoints, feel free to speak publicly what they are privately thinking, ask difficult and even heart-wrenching questions, encourage one another warmly and compassionately, and do not get sucked into a competition for the best grades. In other words, my goal is to grow a Spirit-led learning community. As these qualities grow, the class begins to reflect a sense of godly passion and respect with richer and deeper colors.

Recall the four circles of calling from Chapter Two. God doesn't just call us as individuals—he calls a community to be salt and light in his hurting world. In the same way that two parts hydrogen and one part oxygen (H_2O) do not remain three separate molecules but form something new that we call "water," God calls us into communities that have their own "sanctification chemistry," and each of us is one of the "molecules" that contributes to the shaping of the whole and is in turn shaped by the whole.

Imagine a fictional college grad, Dan Baker, class of '96, business major. Since graduation Dan has saved carefully, and now he's ready to open up his own pizza establishment. The building is ready, the sign proclaiming "Pizza Barn" is up, the ads are out, the employees are hired, and, the afternoon before the grand opening, Dan gathers all the new employees for The Speech:

> Folks, you know that a business needs to make money to stay afloat, but making money isn't my first goal. All my life I've seen how food helps people to enjoy each other's company,

and I see Pizza Barn as a place that helps people enjoy each other's company with the help of good food. I see this as a place of community service. Your job is to prepare great food, always be friendly and hospitable, provide a clean and well-maintained place, and create an atmosphere of good humor. My job is to do all that I can to enable you to do your job well.

Dan knows that some employees will be lazy complainers, some customers will be impossible to please, and mistakes will happen. But his desire is to run a business that is continually being sanctified, reflecting something of the gracious hospitality of God while also providing a service and earning a fair return. Dan sees his job as being in tune with God's sanctifying work as it takes place in his business. He recognizes the importance of group sanctification.

Conclusion

A theme that runs through all of these reflections might be that "the years teach much that the days never know." Sanctification is not about a "quick fix" in which we bring our problems and struggles to the Lord and he pushes the right buttons, takes away our difficulties, and puts on the fast track of becoming Christlike. Just as God's work of redeeming his entire world has been underway for several thousand years, so his work in our own lives and communities is incremental, maturing us bit by bit. Psalm 1 compares maturing in the faith to growing like a tree planted by streams of water. The fastest-growing trees (varieties such as the poplar) are also the weakest, tending to break when the prairie windstorms come howling through. Slow, steady-growing trees are the stronger ones, patiently maturing through the long term, quietly deepening their colors.

Chapter Six

Deepening the Colors

of Our Wisdom

What Is Wisdom?

Practicing habits that encourage God's work of sanctification is part of the Christian life until we die. During the college years, the sanctification of our intellect receives special attention (though learning is a lifelong process). The Bible focuses especially on learning as the formation of *wisdom,* becoming a wiser person. "Wisdom is supreme; therefore get wisdom. Though it cost you all you have, get understanding. Esteem her and she will exalt you; embrace her, and she will honor you" (Proverbs 4:7–8). The writer seems to have had college students in mind when he wrote about the search for wisdom "costing you all that you have," but his advice certainly celebrates the centrality of wisdom in the God-fearing life.

When you think of a wise person, what sort of person comes to mind? I think of a person who is eager to listen and slow to speak, who considers all sides of a matter before coming to a conclusion, and who often will say something startlingly unexpected that makes wonderful sense. When a wise person speaks, the room becomes very silent because everyone present is eager to listen carefully. When I am in the presence of a wise person, I realize that I am too quick to jump to conclusions and too quick to assume that what the majority around me believes must be right.

How would we define wisdom? It's certainly not the same as being "smart" and getting high grades in school. Wisdom has to do with *living well.* A wise person has a deep sense of who God is, how the world works, and what makes people tick; he or she uses that knowledge to make good decisions in specific situations. In other words, a wise person sees the big picture of how things fit together and is able to apply it to hundreds of little pictures day by day. Wisdom does not just involve *what* one knows, but also *who one is* and *how one lives* based on that knowledge.

A wise person is teachable and observant. There's an old proverb that says, "Those can see far who stand on the shoulders of giants." A wise person seeks out wisdom wherever it may be found and learns from it. A wise person observes life, observes what happens to people, what drives them, how their decisions affect them, and filters this observation through the teachings of Scripture and the Christian faith.

Picture two people, one who is fairly wise (Steve) and one who is not (Seymour). Both believe that homosexual behavior is wrong, and neither of them is personally acquainted with anyone who has a homosexual orientation. Rob is a young man who is a friend to both of them, and, after years of struggle, concludes that he is gay and should tell each of his friends.

Seymour hears the news and is both horrified and terrified. He looks at Rob, but he cannot see Rob; all he sees is "gay." He tries to be friendly and encouraging during the conversation, but the conversation is short and, once it's done, he makes no effort to stay in contact with Rob. Dealing with a gay friend is too scary; it forces him to try to understand realities that revolt him, and the Bible condemns it, so he shouldn't have to deal with it. Seymour is too frightened to learn anything, and he uses the Bible to justify his fear and his complete rejection of Rob as a human being.

Steve is also shocked at Rob's revelation, but he recognizes that Rob's struggle has now become his struggle, too, because the stories of their lives are interconnected. He says to Rob,

"I'm not sure what to say. I've never been in this situation be-fore, and I can see how hard it is for you to tell me this. But our friendship is strong enough to handle this news; I'll try to be your friend as you deal with this."

Life is filled with new and unexpected situations. Wisdom is able to draw deep into its wells to find resources for the new and unexpected. Foolishness tries to put blinders on; it pretends that the new and unexpected can be ignored or rejected. Wisdom recognizes that new situations require new ways of applying old answers. For example, the Old Testament teaches that one must not charge interest when lending others money (Leviticus 25:36–37). However, John Calvin noted that these laws made sense in that particular time and place, but in his own day it made more biblical sense to charge a modest rate of interest on loans. In the parable of the Good Samaritan (Luke 10:25–37), the priest and Levite who ignored the injured man were obeying the law because the man looked as though he might be dead, and touching a dead body would disqualify them from religious service. But they did not dare to be wise; they obeyed the written law but disobeyed the deeper laws of love, and this deeper obe-dience requires wisdom because it cannot follow the simple recipes of written laws.

This need for wisdom that is deeper than following laws is il-lustrated many times in the Bible. Sometimes it was ok to eat meat offered to idols (1 Corinthians 8:1–8), and sometimes it was not (Acts 15:29, 1 Corinthians 8:9–13, Revelation 2:20). In some places it was ok for women to exercise leadership in the church (Acts 18:26, Romans 16:1), and in some places it was not (1 Corinthians 14:34, 1 Timothy 2:12). Christians did not need to be circumcised (Acts 15:28, Galatians 5:6), but sometimes it was better for them to do it anyway (Acts 16:3). Christians are expected to get together regularly for worship (Hebrews 10:25), but how they are to worship is not spelled out. Pray continually, we are commanded (1 Thessalonians 5:17), but there are hundreds of different ways to pray. Some Christians celebrate special days and some do not, and Paul gives them this very ambiguous advice: "each one should be fully convinced in his own mind" (Romans 14:5). Clearly, the Bible is not a simple book, and life in God's world is not formulaic. The Christian life requires a great deal of wisdom.

Wisdom-Growing Habits

Wisdom is not a gift or an ability that some folks have and other unfortunate ones lack. If it were, the Bible's encouragements to us to be wise would make no sense. Rather, there are many habits that foster the growth of wisdom. Just a few of these habits are described below.

1. Habits of listening, observing, and noticing.

Hurry is a major enemy of wisdom, and we live in a fast-paced culture. Life feels like a freight train rushing down the track at eighty miles an hour; we'd better jump on or be left behind. There are so many things to do, people to enjoy, movies to watch, deadlines to meet.

Inside this harriedness, we need to cultivate habits of slowing down to listen carefully, observe well, and notice what is happening behind the scenes. Going for walks regularly, forcing oneself to read slowly, writing in a journal, and taking quiet devotional times all grow within us the kind of slowness that frees us up to listen, observe, and notice more fully and deeply. I once attended a retreat where we were told to find a solitary place and spend three hours reading Psalm 23. The Psalm has six verses! I read them in about 53 seconds, and then panicked. Now what do I do for 2 hours, 59 minutes, and 7 seconds? After recovering from my panic, I learned to slow down and enjoy a time of deep refreshment from the wonderful words of that much-beloved Psalm.

Why is slowing down to listen, observe, and notice important for growing in wisdom? In any situation that we are in, any book that we read, any person in our lives, there is always much more there than we immediately are aware of. A life lived on first impressions alone will too easily become shallow, because first impressions often have more to do with our own prejudices and assumptions than what is actually there. Slowing down stretches us to go beyond our own prejudices and assumptions, and the way of wisdom is the way of being stretched. This growing in wisdom is a type of dying to oneself, that is, recognizing that one's initial reactions are never the whole story; we need to learn to hear and see more deeply.

2. Habits of civil discourse.

A common human inclination is to seek out others who share our values, assumptions, and ways of doing things. We are most comfortable with people who are like us. Observers have noted that electronic communication has made it easier to follow this inclination to stay within our comfort zones. Instead of developing relationships with people we meet at work or in class who might be a little different than we are, we can continue long-distance relationships through e-mail and instant messaging with folks who share our views.

Enjoying the company of those like us is a wonderful blessing, but if our human interaction is limited to those like us, our growth in wisdom will suffer. None of us has a perfect understanding of the complexities of life. The way of wisdom holds onto this paradox: on the one hand, I have strong views on many matters and I am personally invested in these views—they mean a great deal to me. On the other hand, I recognize that my views are neither perfect nor final, and that others—even those whose views are the opposite of mine—can be excellent teachers in refining my own views.

Having the grace to be stretched by those who differ from me requires habits of civil discourse. In such conversations, people are free to disagree with each other because they recognize that disagreement is not first of all about a power struggle but rather about a shared desire to grow in wisdom. If you are able to demonstrate a flaw in my thinking, I do not need to be embarrassed; rather, I can be thankful that my own thinking was challenged to become stronger.

There are those who believe that Christians should never disagree with one another because disagreement is not "nice" and doesn't fit with Christlike love. The Bible tells us to love one another, to get along with one another, but it does not say that we must all think in exactly the same way. Conformity kills the growth of wisdom. Conformity assures one of two things: either that the understandings of the entire group will never change and grow or that the powerful leaders of the group will impose their manner of thinking upon the entire group and prevent any challenges to their thinking. Both of these options are wisdom-suffocating.

Habits that encourage the growth of wisdom are all interrelated. Frequently our disagreements are of the "knee-jerk" variety. That is, I spout off opinions based on my prejudices, then you do the same, and then we go at it WWF style until someone is pinned to the floor. In such conversation, the thinking is hurried and true listening and observing rarely take place. As we sometimes say, "that conversation was full of heat without much light." Habits of civil discourse ask probing questions so that we understand the other's view as fully as possible; these habits result in mutual growth.

Habits of civil discourse also require a dying to self. I would rather conclude every conversation being able to say to myself, "Once again, I was totally right and I proved the others wrong." But that desire does not encourage the growth of wisdom. Rather, wisdom invites me to die to myself by acknowledging that I was not completely right and that I have become a stronger person through the good words that were said by another.

3. Habits of critical thinking.

I find it fascinating that when Jesus engaged in teaching he asked many, many questions—questions such as, "Who are my mother and brother and sister?" "Why do you worry about what you shall wear and what you shall eat?" "Which man in the parable was a neighbor to the one in need?" "Do you truly love me?" "Is it better to do good on the Sabbath or to do harm?" "Who do people say that I am?" "Why did you doubt?"

Questions are one of God's greatest gifts to us to grow in wisdom. It has often been said that a primary goal of education is not to give all of the answers but to teach others how to ask the right questions. A good question is like a window; it opens up space in a wall enabling the questioner to see what lies on the other side. A good question allows one to see farther and deeper, to go below the surface.

The opposite of a good question is a hasty conclusion. I hear someone describe his or her view, and I instantly conclude whether I agree or disagree, whether I care or am indifferent. Quick conclusions keep things at a superficial, unexamined level, and they simplify life by not forcing me to change in any way. What I have just heard either reinforces my thinking, so it must be right; or it contradicts it, so it must be wrong; or it's irrelevant and can be ignored.

The habit of critical thinking allows me to die to the unwillingness to examine my own thoughts carefully. When I practice habits of critical thinking, I can see that asking good questions is a skill that I improve in as I practice it, watch others do it, and am taught. I learn to ask questions such as, "Does she mean the same thing with those terms that I mean?" "What assumptions about reality would cause him to write that?" "What unexamined prejudices am I operating from that cause me to discredit that movie so quickly?"

4. Habits of self-reflection.

Self-reflection refers to the activity of processing my own thinking through silent pondering or writing. It takes me out of the whirl of conversation, debate, and activity and gives me space to sort out my thoughts and to allow an inner conversation to continue between myself and what I have heard from others in conversation or through reading. Growing in wisdom always requires some downtime, time when no one else can intrude so that I am free to process in an uninterrupted manner.

It's difficult to find time and space for self-reflection in the twenty-first century. Do you have a room where you can be alone long enough for meaningful self-reflection? In addition to being surrounded by people, we find the distractions of TVs and stereos coming at us from all sides while our e-mail accounts summon us to check for the latest inbox arrivals. Furthermore, there's simply too much to do. Self-reflection feels like wasting time when so many urgent matters are pressing in.

But self-reflection is one of the more urgent activities we can engage in. The Psalmist proclaims it well: "Be still and know that I am God" (Psalm 46:10). In silence, we come to a fuller knowledge of God and, in that knowledge, of ourselves and reality as well. Because most of us write or type more slowly than we think, many people learn habits of self-reflection by journaling their thoughts.

Daydreaming is another wonderful catalyst for self-reflection. I have heard many teachers complaining about students daydreaming too much. The kind of daydreaming that furthers self-reflection is one that takes a particular topic or issue and allows all sides of it—including those that may appear to be weird or even heretical—to be probed, examined, turned upside-down, and "played" with. Through such day-dreaming, a creativity emerges that deepens our thinking and thereby allows wisdom to grow.

5. Habits of postponing perceived relevance.

We have all heard comments and had thoughts like these: "Why do I have to learn this?" "This has no meaning for my life." "This sermon doesn't relate to me at all." "This book is boring and out-of-touch." "Why do I need this course? It contributes nothing to where I'm going."

There is a place for such comments and thoughts. I should know—I've preached sermons that later struck me as marginally helpful at best. But it is usually wise to be cautious about making such comments. Instant relevance means I benefit *right now,* and we need instant relevance in our lives. But I am being sanctified! The colors of my life are being deepened! The contours of my life are not limited to who I am right now, but rather are also defined by *who the Lord is making me to be.* I do not know what he is planning with me, but I do know that he has done his sanctifying work in millions upon millions of others before he came to me, and many of these folks grew to be wiser than I am right now. Therefore, part of my work of trusting in the Lord with all my heart and leaning not on my own understanding is coming to recognize that he has given wisdom to others that I can benefit from *even though I may not understand why it is wisdom right now.* I may read the first chapter of a book and think to myself, "This is boring, I don't need this." But then I decide to allow that thought to die and give the book the benefit of the doubt. I learn to tell myself, "Someone somewhere has found wisdom in this book. I may not see it yet, but I will continue, trusting that eventually it will become clear to me, too."

Once again, this habit is intertwined with all of the others. When I determine that someone is not worth listening to, I will not practice habits of careful listening and I will not feel the need to engage in civil discourse. I will not put energy into critical thinking or reflection. As a result, my initial decision that a person's words cannot benefit me will become a self-fulfilling prophecy: I decided they would be irrelevant, I did not practice any habits that allowed me to find wisdom in them, and, indeed, I did not find any wisdom in them. Perhaps the problem was not in the speaker's words but in me, the listener. I was unwilling to die to myself and postpone the perception of relevance.

These habits for growing in wisdom are obviously another example of a habit cluster. Each one strengthens the other four, and when they are practiced together, bit by bit the practitioner will grow in wisdom, especially as he or she is part of a community that practices such habits.

Chapter Seven

Made in His Image

Ligaments

Do you ever feel as though some parts of your life are much more connected to God than other parts? I often hear people describe others as "Sunday Christians," meaning, "You can tell they are Christians because they go to church on Sunday, but the rest of the week their lives don't look very Christian at all." I've spoken with many people who return from mission trips or service projects all excited about the Lord. After a week or two back on the job or back in school, they often feel confused or discouraged. "I was so connected to God out there on that project, but now I feel far away from him again."

Such struggles are very normal for three reasons. First, our deepest calling is to live as children of God in all that we are and do. Jesus's call to us to "seek first the kingdom" does not have a rider attached to it that says, "and especially on Sundays" or "when you go on mission trips." It's a 24/7 kind of call, and we sense that, so it's very normal that we struggle and feel discouraged when some parts of our lives seem more connected to God than other parts.

Second, one of the marks of a "being-sanctified believer" is that our lives are not yet made whole. There is unevenness in our lives; we will find it easier to follow God's call in some areas of our lives than in other areas. Imagine a basketball star who is known for hitting three-pointers at clutch moments of the game so that his shots serve as momentum turners that deflate the opposing team. His rebounding skills are weaker, and at times, he is caught flat-footed when the other team makes a fast break; his overall game has a kind of unevenness about it, and that's true of many excellent athletes. Similarly, as people walking with Jesus, the sanctification of our lives does not happen with equal power in all that we are and do. When I wrote the previous chapter, it struck me that the sanctification of my intellect is probably stronger than that of my emotions. I'm sure you can notice unevenness in your sanctification, too.

Finally, one of the devil's schemes is to persuade Christians that unevenness is an acceptable part of the Christian life. "You can have Sundays and mission trips," he says, "I'll take care of Monday to Saturday and the daily routines of your life. If you want to do devotions and a couple other habits every day, well, go ahead. That will still leave me the vast majority of your time." In the United States, there are some who interpret the separation of church and state in a manner that fits with this devilish scheme: Christians can worship in their churches as long as they keep their faith hidden inside the private parts of their lives. Because they perceive it as having no bearing in the workplace, in government, in economic matters, in the marketplace, or in entertainment, faith is disconnected from much of life.

Like me, chances are you've never paid much attention to your body's ligaments. Ligaments are "connectors" that hold bones together so that many separate parts of our body function together as one unified whole. Our word *religion* comes from the same root as the word *ligament*. Religion is something that serves as a "reconnector," taking the different parts of our lives and making sense of how they all fit together in a coherent whole. God the Father, the Son, and the Holy Spirit are "religamenters" in our lives, and sanctification is the process through which they do their reconnecting work.

The biblical teaching that points us the most clearly to this work is the teaching concerning the image of God. As we seek to live out our calling as disciples of Jesus, eager to learn the specific ways in which we are called to follow him, understanding how our creation and redemption as the image of God overcomes the unevennesses of sanctification is very helpful.

The Image of God

In Chapter Two, we discussed the image of God in terms of becoming what we worship. This phrase *always* involves identity competition: we are created to reflect God, but we often reflect other, false gods instead. In this chapter, we will see how God created us in his image to connect us to him and his world; that will help us see how our one piece of the jigsaw puzzle fits inside the big picture.

One of the most profound statements the Bible makes about us is that we are created in the image of God. Listen to the Bible's description of our creation:

> Then God said, "let us make man in our image, in our likeness, and let them rule over the fish of the sea and the birds of the air, over the livestock, over all the earth, and over all the creatures that move along the ground." So God created man in his own image, in the image of God he created him; male and female he created them. God blessed them and said to them, "Be fruitful and increase in number; fill the earth and subdue it. Rule over the fish of the sea and the birds of the air and over every living creature that moves on the ground." (Genesis 1:26–28)

The poetic repetition in this passage is a literary way of saying, "This truth is particularly important—sit up and take note!" We can sense that to be human involves a special standing of some sort before the face of God. The second creation account in Genesis 2 does not use the phrase "image of God," but almost the entire chapter focuses on the fashioning of man out of the ground, followed by the fashioning of woman out of man's rib. It presents a deeply loving portrait of a Father-God gently bringing the first man and woman into his creation to tend his garden. Strangely though, these two chapters give no explanation concerning what "image of God" might mean, even though it's clearly one of the most important truths about our identity. As a result, we have to read between the lines and look at other parts of Scripture to gain insight into its meaning.

The phrase "image of God" describes what it is for humans to be situated inside the shalom, the complete harmony, of the creation. Perhaps the Bible says so little about the phrase because shalom is indescribable. Human language can only describe things in pieces and parts; shalom refers to a whole, all-encompassing reality that is far deeper than our words can go. Instead, the Bible provides hundreds of glimpses that describe bits of shalom, and as we fit them together, we begin to sense the whole.

After sin entered God's good world, the only perfect embodiment of the image of God in humankind was Jesus Christ. "He is the image of the invisible God," writes Paul, "the first-born over all creation" (Colossians 1:15). A couple of chapters later, Paul tells us that our sanctification means that we are being restored in the image of God: ". . . you have taken off your old self with its practices, and have put on the new self, which is being renewed in knowledge in the image of its Creator" (Colossians 3:9–10). My old self worships idols and becomes like them. My new self grows toward a very different identity; worshiping God, it becomes more like him, more truly the image of God.

If we survey all of the different ways in which the Bible describes our sanctification in Christ—the deepening of our colors—we find that they can be described in terms of four main categories. These four involve our relationships (1) with God, (2) with our fellow image-bearers, (3) with the whole of creation, and (4) with ourselves (our inner integrity and wholeness). Taken together, these four address the unevennesses of our sanctification because *every part* of our lives falls within these four relationships. We will look at each of these four relationships separately, but they are not distinct from one another: each one affects the other three, and together the four point to the whole picture of shalom surrounding our creatureliness. Each one of these four relationships is affected by cultural dynamics that undermine God's sanctifying, religamenting work in our lives. This entire chapter can be summarized in this one sentence:

Because of God's creating/redeeming work, I am a child of God, partnered with others to rule over his creation with integrity.

Let's unpack that sentence.

Our Relationship with God

First, as people created in the image of God, we are not God—and this "notness" provides wonderful liberation. We are free to be who God created us to be, creatures dependent upon him. The Bible gives us dozens of pictures that describe the way our relationship to God is meant to be, but the deepest one is that we are adopted children of the Father. In the prologue to his gospel, the disciple John tells us that "to all who received him [Jesus], to those who believed in his name, he gave the right to become children of God" (John 1:12). Paul reinforces this theme as he declares that "you did not receive a spirit that makes you a slave again to fear, but you received the spirit of sonship. And by him we cry, 'Abba, Father'" (Romans 8:15).

I am convinced that the greatest challenge of the Christian life is to know deep down in the depths of my bones that I am a child of God. Jesus's most beloved parable, the parable of the prodigal son (Luke 15), describes the father welcoming home his wayward son *as a son,* even though the son had concluded that, at best, he deserved to return only as a hired hand. The son's confusion is our confusion. We are afraid of God, we try to earn favor with God, and we call ourselves "servants of God" because the word *servants* implies that what we *do* for him is what really matters. We are created and redeemed as *children* of the Father, and the word that best describes that relationship is *gift*. "How great is the love the Father has lavished on us, that we should be called children of God! And that is what we are!" (1 John 3:1). Our deepest calling is to accept this gift as helpless children, and it's that word *helpless* that makes it so difficult for us.

But "helpless" does not mean "useless." The dynamic of our relationship with God is that he created and redeemed us, and we *respond*. Because of this dynamic, living as the image of God means that we are *responsible* (i.e., respondable) beings. In our culture, we describe a responsible person as someone who fulfills his or her obligations in a mature and dependable manner. That description comes close, but it loses the bigger picture: God formed us so that we are called to respond to what he did as we reflect him in his world. Or, to put it more directly, he created us so that we would *make a difference in his world in his name*. This world has gone through tremendously dramatic changes since the beginning of time because God has created us with respondability/responsibility. It is as though when God formed us he said, "Go MAD, that is, Go, Make a Difference."

There are three common ways in which that responsibility is misunderstood today. The first is found among Christians. "God is completely in control," they think, "and therefore we cannot make a difference, we cannot be responsible." Often the Christian teachings of election and predestination are misinterpreted in this way to diminish human responsibility. The Bible abounds with accounts describing how human responsibility makes a difference for good or for ill throughout history, with hundreds of encouragements to listen to the Lord's call because he takes our responsibility so seriously. One of my favorites is found in Philippians 2:

> Continue to work out your salvation with fear and trembling, for it is God who works in you to will and to act according to his good purpose. Do everything without complaining or arguing, so that you may become blameless and pure, children of God without fault in a crooked and depraved generation, in which you shine like stars in the universe as you hold out the word of life (vv. 12–16).

Follow the sequence of Paul's encouragement: (1) you are responsible to work out your salvation (2) as you respond to God who is working in you, (3) so that you will make a difference by shining like stars in a very dark world.

A second misunderstanding sees responsibility as a burden, something that makes our lives difficult and caged in. To have responsibility is the opposite of having fun, and a responsible person is probably a boring person. The biblical sense of responsibility is much more liberating and playful. For example, I am convinced that the Lord has called me to teach, and I respond to his call by teaching at a Christian college. On those days when teaching goes well, it is a complete joy to be able to carry out these responsibilities—I am filled with a sense of freedom, purpose, and, yes, I even have a lot of fun. On such days, I resonate completely with the words of the normally gloomy writer of Ecclesiastes: "I saw that there is nothing better for a man than to enjoy his work, because that is his lot" (Ecclesiastes 3:22).

The third misunderstanding comes from our culture's emphasis on human autonomy. According to this theme, if I am responsible, then I must be in charge, independent. Autonomy literally means "self-law"—I am the one who decides what is right or wrong, true or false, important or insignificant. Former Minnesota governor Jesse Ventura said it well when he claimed that Christianity was for weaklings. According to our culture, some people may need to depend on a god to make it through life;

truly responsible people make it on their own. They are strong, individualistic, self-driven, independent human beings. While the Christian sees the white flag of surrender as a symbol of giving all to the Father, the culture cries out, "Never surrender. Fight for yourself to the end." A Christian understanding of responsibility rests in living as a dependent child of the Father, not in seeking autonomy.

Our Relationships with Fellow Image-Bearers

Sometimes Christians are tempted to stop after this first point. Our relationship to God is the most important dimension of our lives, they reason, and once we've described it the rest is far less important. "Get right with God" and everything else will take care of itself. In a sense that's true, but in another sense, it's very misleading. Shalom refers to *everything* in the right place in every way; Western Christianity has a history of practicing compartmentalization. I divide up my life into different "boxes"; I have a "faith" box and a "career" box and a "citizenship" box and they don't have that much to do with each other. If we agree that getting right with God is all that matters, we may well be tempted to make sure our "God" box is right and let the other boxes go their own way. Our religion does not do its "ligamenting" work.

John highlights this problem in his first epistle. He writes, "If anyone says, 'I love God,' yet hates his brother, he is a liar. For anyone who does not love his brother, whom he has seen, cannot love God, whom he has not seen" (1 John 4:20). Here John points us to a second principal dimension of living in the image of God: living in right relationship with others. The creation accounts already point us in this direction. "In the image of God he created him, male and female he created them" (Genesis 1:27b) suggests that in their partnership, the man and woman shared in the image of God. After creating the man, God reflects on his creation and concludes, "It is not good for the man to be alone. I will make a helper suitable for him" (Genesis 2:18). Imagine that—Adam is created and lives in perfect fellowship with God, and God concludes that this perfect fellowship is not enough! To be whole, to rest in shalom, man also needs interpersonal relationships. And God gives him the gift of woman.

Genesis 2 ends with a description of marriage, a particularly intense form of human relationship, but when we look at Scripture as a whole we realize that we are not required to be married to live out the image of God. Paul contrasts marriage with singleness in 1 Corinthians 7, and, though he has chosen the latter, he recognizes that each has a legitimate place in God's world. To live as the image of God means that we were created to need other people and others were created to need us, a reality that we can call "loving interdependence."

When I ask my students to point out factors that have helped them grow in their walk with God, almost everyone will mention others who have helped them by their example, their words, their friendship, books they have written, or songs they have performed. Without other people to share in our joys and sorrows, encourage us when we are down, advise us when we are confused, and just plain love us as we love them, life would seem barren and empty. A missionary in the third world once mentioned that he felt a little guilty because every morning he checked his e-mail before he did his devotions. Should he feel guilty? I don't think so. We are created to need God and to need other people, and we cannot separate those two needs.

The sequence doesn't matter because these two aspects of the image of God are completely intertwined. We can't live as dependent children of the Father if we are not living as interdependent partners of one another. It's hard for us to acknowledge our neediness, but as we say to the Lord, "I can't live without you," we find it easier to say the same words to others, and as we recognize our need for others, we also grow in giving our neediness to the Lord. Remember how frequently the Bible intertwines these two relationships. We are taught to pray, "forgive us our debts, as we also have forgiven our debtors" (Matthew 6:12). The forgiveness that makes us right with God only "takes" as we forgive others and so become right with them as well. Jesus says that when we feed the hungry, clothe the naked, and visit the sick we are really doing it all to him (Matthew 25:40). Biblical metaphors that describe our relationship to God also describe our relationship to one another. Jesus is the vine, we are branches (John 15); he is the head, and we are all parts of an interconnected body (1 Corinthians 12); he is the cornerstone and foundation, and we are all stones in the temple (Ephesians 2, 1 Peter 2).

The Western cultural ideal of human autonomy also undermines this second dimension of the image of God. The autonomous human individual who does not need God does not need other people either. We tend to define maturity as learning to stand on your own two feet, not needing the help of others any more, and being able to make your own decisions. Crying is a sign of weakness and should not be done in the presence of others (especially if you are male). In contrast, the Bible describes mature faith as becoming like a child (Matthew 18:3–4), letting go to trust in God and to acknowledge our interdependence with others.

One specific area where the tension between the Bible's story and our culture's story comes into very clear focus is the area of mutual accountability. One implication of the statement "it is not good for man to be alone" is that we need others to keep us on the right path; we need others to keep us accountable, and others need us. That mutual accountability has become an extremely difficult skill for Christians to practice in a cultural context that preaches the "gospel" of individualism, autonomy, and tolerance. "Judge not" is the Bible verse that we focus on, forgetting that Jesus doesn't tell us to ignore others' struggles. Rather, he reminds us to take the plank out of our own eye before we help a neighbor take the speck out of his or her eye (Matthew 7:1–5). Mutual accountability is one of the strongest activities to help us grow with the Lord (get right with God), and therefore it's no surprise that our culture's story so deeply undermines our ability to practice this habit. It simply illustrates again how thoroughly intertwined these two dimensions of living as the image of God are.

Our Relationship with the Creation

The phrase *image of God* also has tremendous implications in a third area: our relation to the entire creation. No other creature of the Lord is identified as being in the image of God. Therefore, the phrase tells us important truths concerning how we as human beings fit in with the shalom that filled the entire creation and its relation to God. The first two chapters of Genesis provide several clues concerning the character of this relationship. First, they describe our activity in God's world. We read, "Then God said, 'Let us make man in our image, in our likeness, and let them rule over the fish of the sea and the birds of the air, over the livestock, over all the earth, and over all creatures that move along the ground'" (Genesis 1:26). After the creation of Adam and Eve, we find a restating of these words, "God blessed them, and said to them, 'Be fruitful and increase in number, fill the earth and subdue it. Rule over the fish of the sea and the birds of the air and over every living creature that moves on the ground'" (Genesis 1:28). The first statement is simply passive/descriptive, but the second is active/prescriptive, what we might call an "active blessing." This is the first call to action recorded in Scripture, and this call is elaborated upon in Genesis 2. "The Lord God took the man and put him in the Garden of Eden to work it and take care of it" (Genesis 2:15); part of this care included naming the animals that the Lord God brought to him (vv. 19–20).

The key to understanding this third dimension of living as image-bearers is found in the word *rule*. How are we to understand what it means to rule over the creation? The blessing clearly suggests that we are called to work with God's creation to make it fruitful and productive, but how do we do that? Our culture's story, grounded in human autonomy, defines "rule" to mean "Do as you please. Run the show in a way that works best for you." The result is an attitude that reaps as much benefit from the creation as possible without much regard for our effect upon the creation. Natural resources are there for the taking, and thanks to them we (at least, many North Americans) enjoy lives of abundant plenty. This state of ruling has discovered that heavy fertilization makes lands more productive, confinement lots make beef production more efficient, and third-world factories provide cheaper labor and lower pollution standards. It seems to work for us in the short term, and we are all that really matters.

During the past twenty years, many voices (both Christian and non-Christian) have protested this manner of ruling. One response has been to shift completely in the opposite direction: Because giving human beings a privileged place in creation has led to the abuse of creation, we must remove this privileged place. All creatures are of equal value; a tree, a whale, a human being are all of equal worth, and one should never be sacrificed for the sake of another. Animals should not be used for scientific research that is seeking to cure human diseases; trees should not be felled to produce lumber for human construction. The pendulum swings the other way and the concepts of humans ruling over creation is completely abandoned.

Neither of these extremes makes biblical sense. Instead, it's helpful to allow the entire Bible to describe for us what ruling looks like in God's world. To rule is to exercise authority the way God exercises authority, and we see the glory of God most clearly in the face of Jesus Christ (2 Corinthians 4:6). One of the most moving stories in the gospels occurs shortly before the crucifixion of Jesus. Just before an intimate Passover meal with his disciples, Jesus gets up from the table and washes his disciples' feet, thereby taking on the task normally assigned to the lowest slave in the household. After he is finished, he explains his actions: "You call me 'Teacher' and 'Lord,' and rightly so, for that is what I am. Now that I, your Lord and Teacher, have washed your feet, you also should wash one another's feet" (John 13:13–14). Frequently we hear Jesus's ministry described as servant-authority, the exercise of authority in ways that serve the best interests of those he is ruling over. Or, to put it another way, his way of exercising authority leads to restored shalom and deepened colors. The foot-washing story is not an isolated event but is the clearest example of a pattern that typifies the rule of Jesus.

Human rule over the creation is meant to be a servant-authority; we work in God's creation to restore and deepen shalom in any way possible. The creation provides us with food and shelter, and plants, animals, trees, and many other materials are able to contribute to these needs. But we are able to receive these gifts from the creation in such a way that creation's fruitfulness is enhanced, not lessened.

To the best of our knowledge, the original hearers of Genesis 1 were Hebrew slaves who had been liberated from Egypt by the mighty hand of the Lord. Their experience of rule came at the oppressive hands of Pharaoh. Most of them had never met

Pharaoh, but he placed his image all over Egypt where the slaves worked to remind them that he was the authority there even though he was not physically present. Others exercised authority in his name.

Now it is as though the Lord says to these liberated slaves, "You experienced rule in an abusive way, administered by supervisors standing under the image of Pharaoh. Instead, you are called to rule over the entire creation, and you are in my image, ruling in my name and on my behalf. Rule in a way that fits with who I am, the sovereign and gracious creator of all." God is the ultimate ruler over the creation, but he delegates rule to us so that we rule in his name, in a very uneven partnership with him.

As we rule over the creation, we participate in *cultural formation*. Cultural formation refers to every form of human activity. We get married and raise families, we devise ways of governing ourselves, we seek the best ways to meet our needs for survival—the need for food, clothing, shelter. We develop patterns of worship, patterns of entertainment, patterns of producing and consuming goods. We develop understandings of what it means to be male and female, young and old. We educate ourselves and establish criteria for determining what should be included in a good education. We articulate laws and justice systems and seek to implement these in various ways. In thousands of ways, humankind expresses this dimension of the image of God by engaging in cultural formation. The forms that this takes vary in different cultural contexts—that is, in different times and places—but underlying these uniquenesses, we find common human needs and desires. For example, the definition of a good, healthy marriage changes from place to place and time to time, but marriage is found in all human cultures.

One might say that ruling over creation involves discovering two gifts: the gifts that are hidden within the creation and the gifts for exploration and development that are hidden within ourselves. It works in this way: the creation is filled with almost limitless potential waiting to be found and developed. There are songs waiting to be composed, technologies waiting to be invented, new ways of teaching waiting to be developed, and on and on. It's staggering to ponder how much has already been explored to this point in human history, but many more opportunities are waiting. No human being is capable of doing all of the work of exploration and development. Instead, God has given each of us different gifts for ruling over his creation, and part of our task of following him is discerning which gifts we have for exploring the gifts in the creation. The gifts within and the gifts without work together as we exercise rule in God's world.

We've noted how Jesus helps us to understand the character of ruling in God's world. It is also helpful to note how the three aspects of the image of God we have discussed to this point are intertwined. We are dependent children of a gracious Father, and as children we receive all of the goodness of the creation as a gift from his hand. Our dependence upon him places us in a posture of humility, receptiveness, and gratitude; and that posture shapes how we approach his creation as well. The blessings of creation are not things that we own to do with as we please; they are gifts of grace that we receive with thanksgiving and use in ways that honor the Father's rule over his entire creation.

Similarly, we rule over the creation as people who are mutually interdependent. We cannot develop the entire creation on our own; perhaps I have gifts to make music, and I share my gift with others as I am blessed by their gifts of providing food, health care, good government, sound teaching, and so on. This interdependence has become structured through human institutions. I need others to receive a good post–secondary education, and colleges have been founded as institutions to enable people to work together to provide such education. I need others to maintain the roads that I drive on, enforce the laws that protect me, and maintain standards for health care; governments function as institutions that enable people to work together to provide these (and many other) benefits.

I know that I am called to develop the gifts that God has placed within me, but it can be terribly confusing to know and discern what those gifts are! I need others to help me see what I do well, where my passions lie, what fits with who God is making me to be, and what does not fit. During my years as a college student, I was convinced that I could never have been called to teach. In my senior year, I began to change my mind, and I remembered then that several years earlier I had been explaining something to a cousin and I overheard my aunt say to my mother, "He's very good at explaining things; maybe he'll make a good teacher some day." Sentences like that are like little seeds that, when planted, help us to discern our gifts.

Every course and every major at college supports in some way the process of discerning and developing the gifts God has given us to understand, develop, and use the gifts in his creation. In other words, what we do in our classes seeks to strengthen the image of God within us. Agriculture explores God's gifts in the fruitfulness of the land, and education looks at ways in which God has created us to learn and teach. Social work recognizes that, because of sin, many human situations are not the way God intended them to be and studies God's gifts of healing for brokenness. Business courses work with the dynamics of providing goods and services. We could go on and on. Name a course or a major, and one can describe how it relates to ruling the creation in the name of the Lord.

Inner Integrity and Wholeness

There's one final area of the image of God to discuss: inner integrity and wholeness. The image of God does not refer to a particular part or aspect of our humanness; rather, our totality, all that we are, a human life in perfect harmony, comprises the image of God. This point needs to be made because throughout history, some Christians have identified a *part* of our human creatureliness as somehow being more "religious" or more "spiritual" than the rest and have therefore assumed that this part was really what the image of God was all about. For example, some Christians have said that our soul has to do with the image of God and that our bodies do not, because souls are considered to be eternal, bodies temporary, and the fact that we have souls ultimately distinguishes us from all other creatures. At times, Christians have equated soul with mind and have concluded that our intellect somehow reflects the image of God and that other parts of us (especially our emotions and appetites) are lesser parts that cannot image God. A related view suggests that men are more intellectual than women; therefore, men are more true representations of the image of God than women are. All of these views are influenced by the compartmentalization that we discussed earlier. Scripture supports none of them.

Instead, our entire being is called to walk as the image of God, and all of the different aspects of our being are called to live in harmony with one another in reflecting that image. We are called to inner integrity and wholeness. Because of sin, none of us experiences that kind of complete harmony. We sense our emotions struggling with our intellect, bodily desires fighting against our beliefs, actions that do not fit with our sense of right and wrong, dreams and desires that do not match with our actions. I know a child who had a fervent dream to become a goalie in the National Hockey League; he prayed about this dream almost every night when he went to bed. But he felt no need to practice, to learn the skills that are essential to success, to work over and over again to become the best that he could be. His parents just smiled, but we can recognize a pattern here that we all struggle with. We live with disconnections between different parts of our being. We were created to have all of the parts of our being in complete harmony, like a team of eight horses pulling a stagecoach, but that's very difficult for us to do. Living as the image of God puts us on the road of seeking to have our entire being reflect the glory of God.

I experience conflict inside myself much of the time. For example, after I have taught a class that did not go that well, I find myself thinking, "Hielema, are you sure you're meant to be a teacher? You had nothing to say today and your students clearly knew it. Quit now before you become a total failure." In the solitude of my office after a miserable hour of teaching, the sanctification of my "insides" can kick in. I realize that my thinking is completely focused on one hour of my life and that such a narrow focus tends to be blinded by self-absorption. As my range of vision widens beyond that one hour, I remember many times in my life that my calling to teach was confirmed. I remember many times returning to my office after class knowing that the hour completed had been a good one. I remember that as a being-sanctified child of God, my life will inevitably carry many unevennesses, including having a bad day (or even a bad month) in the classroom. And these rememberings tell me that tomorrow (or the next month) will be better. I can go on with peace and joy in my heart—even on a bad day—because I am part of the big picture of God's way with his world. When a bad day hits, I need to reflect upon it and ask myself what I might do to improve things, but that reflection occurs inside a picture frame, and on the frame are written the words, "I am a child of God on the road of sanctification with him—take heart, and 'keep on keeping on' with him."

Conclusion: The Rainbow of Shalom

The image of God is the central defining phrase that tells us who we are and how we are to live in relation to the entirety of God's creation and the Lord himself. The phrase defines what shalom looks like in human life. Shalom filled the creation that the good Lord had made—like light. When that shalom-light "hit" humankind and filtered through it as though it were a prism, that shalom emerged as a four-colored rainbow displaying the four principal ways in which we reflect the glory of God: by living as children of the Father, partners with one another, rulers over creation, and doing it all with inner integrity and wholeness.

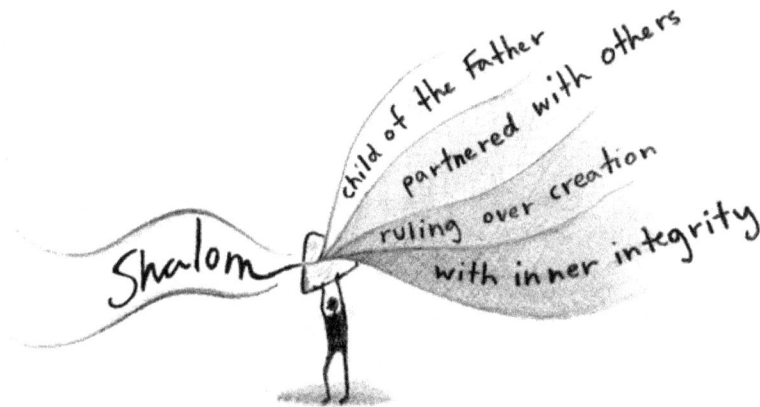

We can see the separate colors of the rainbow, but we cannot pull these colors apart. Whenever one color becomes truer and deeper, the other colors deepen as well. When I mature as a child of God, surrendering my life to him and trusting in him, I more easily recognize that I need other people, that my "ruling" over God's creation is to be done as a respectful servant, and that God desires all of me to surrender to him. My faith grows as I pray and read the Scriptures, but my faith also grows when *any* of these four colors are deepened. When I can discern what gifts God has given me and am able to use them in his world, I am strengthened as a child of God. When I lead a balanced life, avoiding the extremes of workaholism or partyism that are so prevalent, my inner integrity grows and I am strengthened as a child of God. When I cultivate meaningful relationships with others, engaging in real conversation and participating in good projects with them, I am strengthened as a child of God. The beauty of living in the image of God is that it can be strengthened through every single aspect of our lives.

Even so, I am tempted to compartmentalize my faith and lose sight of the whole picture. I have a friend who for a time in his life spent two hours doing devotions every morning before he went to work. It finally came to a point where his wife was unable to speak with him until he came home from work because his quiet time with God could not be disturbed in the morning. As a result, his marriage began to suffer. He assumed that his wife would realize that time with God had obvious priority, and he could catch up with her later in the day if his work didn't tire him out too much. She felt demeaned, as though she was only worthy of receiving the leftovers. Eventually he realized that she was right. Being strengthened in the Lord is not about ignoring other responsibilities. Rather, it is seeing the calling of the Lord in all that we do and all that we are. It is deepening all of the colors, not just one.

God's gift of the Holy Spirit is like an "image of God color-deepener." One of my favorite descriptions of the Spirit's work is found in Galatians 5:22–23, where Paul writes, "The fruit of the Spirit is love, joy, peace, patience, kindness, goodness, faithfulness, gentleness, and self-control." Imagine a person who matures with this kind of fruit. Such a person will rest more fully in the love of

God as his child, finding peace and joy by trusting in him. Such a person becomes more fit for community because love, patience, kindness, faithfulness, and self-control are wonderful aids for growing interpersonal relationships. Such a person becomes a wiser ruler over a little corner of God's creation because she has the patience to discern what her gifts are and the goodness to seek what is best for God's world rather than running toward the first career that promises a fat paycheck. Such a person grows in inner integrity; yes, she may experience all kinds of inner conflicts, but these inner conflicts rest inside peace and gentleness, which smooth her rough, jarring edges. Such a person is growing toward being the kind of image-bearer God intended.

We are called to be the image of God all of the time—in all that we do and are. Therefore, we can look at any moment of our lives and see the four colors of the rainbow dancing together. I'll end this chapter with an example from my own life.

A habit that I enjoy is watching the news with my family after dinner, a habit that I experience as a wonderful image of God color-deepener. I watch the news because the earth is the Lord's and the fullness thereof, and I am convinced that as his responsible child I need to know what is happening in this hurting world that he loves so much. I find that most news on television is superficial, treating me as a consumer whose attention must be held through the next set of commercials. The news that we watch with our family, however, contains a commercial-free full hour of in-depth analysis that practices all of the habits that encourage wisdom (described in the previous chapter). In other words, this news program treats me like a responsible being made in the image of God. I watch because I am his child and those things that concern the Father are also of concern to me—rainbow color #1.

I love watching it with my family. We make comments to each other as we watch, helping each other understand and digest

what we see and hear. Our comments may describe our emotional reactions to what is going on, or we may bring in other bits of information that we have heard that will further our understanding of what is going on. A common term today is "compassion fatigue," that is, people see so much news about trouble in the world that they become numb to it; they become apathetic and would rather not be aware of the news at all. I find that sharing reactions to the news with my family provides a helpful antidote to compassion fatigue. Various news items work their way into our dinnertime prayers every day as well, so the news-watching habit is reinforced by the dinnertime prayer habit, and vice versa, and both of these habits involve the entire family—rainbow color #2.

I need to watch the news because I am called to rule over the creation. The rule that I am part of is primarily very local (my immediate environs), so why do I need to watch in-depth news analysis of the Middle East, Africa, and other remote regions? I need to watch because we live in a global village; the actions of my country have a tremendous effect in every part of the earth, and I am responsible—in part—for the actions of my country. Furthermore, how I live my life in my home town is affected by major events thousands of miles away. When I notice that many nations on earth perceive America to be a bully nation that imposes its will upon others to protect its own interests, then I recognize that my life is called to reflect a God who calls his people to live lives that do not put their own interests first and that are shaped by gentleness and patience. There are many connections between the "small-scale" rule that I exercise and the "large-scale" ruling that takes place all over the earth— rainbow color #3.

Finally, watching the news strengthens my inner integrity and wholeness. Being aware of major global events puts my life inside a bigger picture and challenges me to expand my local experiences. I can become bogged down with fairly trivial personal matters; seeing the big picture helps me to reorganize my priorities in a more godly way. Yes, I promised my wife I'd pick up some groceries and my son hasn't cleaned up his room yet, but these concerns are placed alongside the African AIDS epidemic, Israeli-Palestinian hostilities, and the global struggle against terrorism. They all matter, and part of godly living involves sorting them all out inside my being—rainbow color #4.

This rainbow analysis of watching the news is, in some ways, just plain absurd. We don't go through life looking for rainbow colors everywhere. But there's a point to this absurdity: we are the image of God *all of the time*. Being his image is not something we put on when we go to church, do devotions, or carry out random acts of kindness. When we come to see these four colors of the rainbow interacting with each other in every part of our lives, we are "religamented," we will grow to maturity in Christ more fully, and we will truly be deepening our colors.

Chapter Eight

"So What

Am I S'posed to Do?"

Pilgrim's Progress at the Grand Canyon

Our family hiked part of the Grand Canyon recently. The last leg of the return up to the rim was a sheer cliff about two hundred feet high. From a distance, it looked impossible to climb. But closer up we could see the path winding back and forth eight times across the cliff face, with each loop of the path rising about twenty-five feet. It took a while to get to the top and its magnificent view over the entire canyon, but the climb itself was not that strenuous. I had to smile as I stood at the bottom of that cliff and looked up at various groups of hikers on each of the path's eight loops: some were exhaustedly trudging to the finish line, while others were joking and carrying on as though nothing could be easier. The picture brought to mind a community of pilgrims slowly but surely making their way to their life's destination.

The question, "So what I am supposed to do with my life?" is like that path. From a distance, it can feel like looking at a cliff that I am called to climb. The "answer" seems to be hidden just over the rim at the top, where God can see it but I can't. It feels as though I will need mountain climbing gear and world-renowned Sherpa guides to get me up there, but then I notice a long and winding path cut into the cliff face. I say to myself, "The cliff is 200 feet high; when I add up the total distance of the eight loops that are cut into the cliff, I see that I will be walking 2,000 feet to climb 200 feet. Is it worth it to walk all that extra distance?" Then I realize how silly those thoughts are. I don't need expensive equipment and even more expensive guides; instead, the Lord has fashioned the climb so that the questions that are raised on each leg of the looping path will gradually lead me through the "s'posed to do" questions.

The goal of this book has been to traverse that long and winding path. We began with the questions, "What is the kingdom of God? What does it mean that I am called to seek first the kingdom?" As I start up the trail, these questions make me nervous at first; it feels overwhelming to place all of my life under the rule of the king and the umbrella of his kingdom. But then I realize that the Lord is providing me a way to prioritize my life, a way to make sense of it with him at the center. When my search for a career, a church community, a spouse, volunteer work, and everything else consciously happens inside the coming of his kingdom, I come to see my life is part of something that is much bigger than me. It's not about me, it's about the King and his kingdom. He is making all things new, and I am asked to participate in the renovations. Seeking first the kingdom in all that I am and do is overwhelming, but I remember Jesus's promise, "Do not be afraid, little flock, for your Father has been pleased to give you the kingdom" (Luke 12:32). The seeking is grace-filled; I do not walk alone.

On the second loop, we noted that the "what am I supposed to do" question is a "God question" that zooms out like an expanding lens to raise bigger questions such as, "Who am I called to be? How am I part of the Christian community? How do I hear God's call to his entire world?" The kingdom umbrella always challenges me to look at the biggest picture possible. I stop for a moment on the trail and look out over the Grand Canyon; its breathtaking beauty never fails to astound me, but I also notice the erosion, the dryness, the scorching heat. A circling hawk is searching for a mouse to eat, and I remember the carcasses we have seen during our hike: incredible wonder and deep groaning intertwined. My walk continues with God—immersed in his world, surrounded by his people. Through all of these connections, I grow to be who the Lord intends to me to be.

As I continue climbing, I hear the call to become a new person in Christ, to put off the old self and put on the new through lifelong sanctification, to become truly myself and deepen the colors the Lord is painting in me. I become easily discouraged on this hike; there is so much "old entanglement" that hinders me and won't let go! The top of the cliff still looks so far away. But between me and the rim (as well as below me) I see dozens of others. "Therefore, since we are surrounded by such a great cloud of witnesses, let us throw off everything that hinders and the sin that so easily entangles, and let us run with perseverance the race marked out for us. Let us fix our eyes on Jesus, the author and perfecter of our faith" (Hebrews 12:1–2). With that encouragement, I notice that many people on the trail are practicing "truth-walking habits" that help them to persevere: they lean slightly forward as they walk uphill, they use a walking stick, they encourage each other, and they pause after each loop to drink from their water bottles before continuing. But some on the trail practice detrimental habits: in too much of a hurry, they run and wear themselves out; they slip, kicking loose rocks that begin to roll down the cliff and injure those below; they complain about the heat, about other travelers, and about how far away the rim still seems to be.

I've arrived at the fourth loop, and I am reminded that God claims every part of my being, every aspect of my life. My faithfulness on this trail requires my mind to be sharp, my body fit, my emotions in tune, my desires focused, my actions appropriate, my relationships mutually supportive. I look up and the rim seems to be no closer. That's the trouble with a gradually ascending trail: you hardly notice yourself making any progress. I don't *feel* as though my intellect, emotions, desires, or anything else are being sanctified in significant ways. But then I look below me and realize that I actually have come quite a distance on those first three loops. I remember my life four or five years ago, and yes, I have grown in the Lord! He *has* begun a good work in me, and he *will* bring it to completion (Philippians 1:6). I *am* being made new in Christ. I *will* keep on putting one foot ahead of the other along this trail.

I come to the fifth loop and pause to look over the Grand Canyon again. Its kingdom perspective floods over me; as I breath in the scenery along with the fresh air, I remember that God calls me to be more deeply human. But that sounds so vague: aren't we all human already? I remember how easy it is for us mortals to exhibit horrible inhumanity. I am called to be *fully* human as Jesus was fully human; I have been redeemed to deepen the image of God that I am. I am called to be a child of the Father, partnered with others to rule over his world with integrity. Such a short sentence, but it infiltrates every corner of my life! It seems to sum up every loop that I've traveled so far. Gradually that feeling of being overwhelmed is covered by a comforting assurance: *I am his child.* Yes, I have a long way to go, but it's ok. He is walking with me, and his rod and his staff will comfort me. Often his rod and his staff come in the form of others in my life, and our Father entrusts us together to rule over his world in his name. I still have many questions concerning the details of who the others are and what the ruling means, but as I walk this path I'm beginning to trust that those questions will be resolved at the right time, because that's how a Father walks with his children.

So I keep on walking, remembering encouraging words from the apostle Paul: "I press on to take hold of that for which Christ Jesus took hold of me. Forgetting what is behind, and straining toward what is ahead, I press on toward the goal to win the prize for which God has called me heavenward in Christ Jesus" (Philippians 3:12–14).

Calling or Plan?

The "So what am I s'posed to do?" question is a *walking* question, but we tend to turn it into a *paralyzing* question. It immobilizes us if we think we need answers before we start walking.

The question especially becomes paralyzing when we change it to ask, "What is God's plan for my life?" Those who ask this question picture God's plan as a book that tells the story of my life from conception to death; written on its pages are the names of my spouse and my children, the various career paths I should follow, the places where I will live, and even what I will eat for breakfast on July 17, 2016. God has all of the details right there in the book, and my job is to discern what's on each page and follow the script. When I have that picture in my mind, it's as though I'm standing at the bottom of the cliff, the answers are up there at the top, and somehow I must figure out those answers before I can begin the climb. I am paralyzed.

This approach is based on a misunderstanding of Scripture, and in particular, of two commonly quoted verses. When the Old Testament people of Judah are in exile, Jeremiah brings them this good word: "'For I know the plans I have for you,' declares the Lord, 'plans to prosper you and not to harm you, plans to give you hope and a future'" (Jeremiah 29:11). This verse's promise of a planned-out, hope-filled future for God's people thousands of years ago provides wonderful assurance and comfort still today. Many people have told me that this is their favorite Bible verse and that it's especially comforting when tragedy strikes. I've heard comments such as, "I don't know why my best friend was killed in that car accident, but I know it was part of God's plan, and 'in all things God works for the good of those who love him'" (Romans 8:28).

Does this Jeremiah verse really support the picture of God holding a book containing his plan for all of the details of my life? The verse tells us that God's plan for his people includes four things: prosperity, freedom from harm, hope, and a future. We might paraphrase the Lord's words here by saying, "Now you are in exile and life looks bleak, but I promise you that things will go well for you, for I will always be faithful to you." The word *plan* here points to a *promise* that is intended to provide assurance, comfort, and hope. Exile is an experience of abandonment, and God is saying, "You may feel abandoned, but you are not. I am with you and you will be held in my hands." The sense of the verse is not so much that God is calling his people to focus on a book of plans that he may be holding, but that he is reminding them of his *character,* assuring them that though their situation has changed, he has not changed. He is and will always be the faithful one, and therefore they can continue walking with him even though they are living in exile.

Another commonly quoted passage is Psalm 139:15–16: "My frame was not hidden from you when I was made in the secret place. When I was woven together in the depths of the earth, your eyes saw my unformed body. All the days ordained for me were written in your book before one of them came to be." The Jeremiah verse is addressed to an entire community, while David's psalm is intensely personal. David refers very clearly to a "book," which sounds like the book that records all of the details of my life from its beginning ("when I was woven together in the depths of the earth") to its end. But the Psalm does not encourage us to focus us on figuring out the details of this book. Rather, the Psalmist—like Jeremiah—points us to the astounding character of God, the sovereign Lord of the universe who is with me—insignificant little me—no matter where I go. Every moment of my life is lived *Coram Deo,* before the face of God. Once again, it's as though we can hear the biblical writer singing,

"Great is thy faithfulness." That's why David ends the Psalm with these words: "Search me, O God, and know my heart; test me and know my anxious thoughts. See if there is any offensive way in me, and lead me in the way everlasting" (Psalm 139:23–24). David ends with a *walking* prayer; he asks the Lord to lead him on the right path.

Misunderstanding the meaning of God's plan tends to become somewhat paradoxical: on the one hand, God's plan fills me with assurance, comfort, and a sense of purpose, and it shows me that God's love is present in the details of my life. Scripture supports understanding God's presence in our lives in that way. On the other hand, assuming that it's our job to figure out God's plan for our lives can make us very anxious: what if I get it wrong? What if he dropped a hint or gave a sign and I missed it? God is like the third base coach; he told me to drop down a suicide squeeze bunt, but I missed the sign and thought it was a hit and run play. Suddenly his presence in my life doesn't seem nearly as comforting.

The paradox can be put another way by contrasting God's plan with God's call: *calling* is a term that assumes a *conversation* between a personal God and his creation. God calls: I listen, respond, and follow in the context of a personal relationship. In Scripture, Christians are identified as those who are "called into fellowship with Jesus Christ" (1 Corinthians 1:8) and urged "to live lives worthy of God, who calls [believers] into his kingdom and glory" (1 Thessalonians 2:12). To be called is to be personally connected, to walk in conversation with God.

Speaking of God's plan, by contrast, is impersonal. God becomes more like my observer or my judge than my conversation partner. I must first become the "decoder" who figures out what's written in the book, and then I become the "performer" who must get it right. Just as the serpent in Genesis 3 distorted Eve's understanding about God and about herself, so understanding God's plan in this way distorts the character both of God and of ourselves. Instead of interacting with God, we interact with his plan; God becomes the detached observer checking to see how we do, and we become anxious detectives searching for clues and trying to fit them together.

A plan is all about *doing;* a call is first of all about *being*—it pulls me into a relationship that shapes who I am. God's call to me is to come to him and be his child, to rest in his great love for the world (John 3:16), to trust in him with all of my heart and acknowledge him in all of my ways (Proverbs 3:5), together with the Christian community that lives in God's groaning creation. In that context, we can begin to discern what we will do.

Implications of Calling

We began this book by noting that when we ponder our calling we are easily tempted to rush to the question, "What am I called to do?" Now that we have come

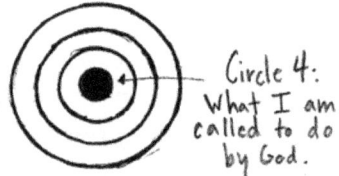

Circle 4: What I am called to do by God.

a long way in our zigzagging path up the Grand Canyon, we can begin to work with the "to do" question. I have found the following guidelines helpful as I walk with the Lord as his child, seeking to understand what he would have me do:

1. There is often more than one obedient option.

Imagine that a parent says to a teenage son, "I'm not feeling well at all today; would you please prepare dinner for the family?" The son agrees and then must decide what to prepare: will it be mac and cheese or grilled burgers? He knows that he can do a good job at either one, and that the family will enjoy both equally well. It's a beautiful summer afternoon, so he decides to grill some burgers.

In this case, obedience involved the son recognizing the neediness of the parent's situation and his ability to lovingly take care of one aspect of family life. The specific details of exactly how he was obedient were secondary. If the son had decided to make a meal that he loved but everyone else in the family disliked, his choice would not have been disobedient but it would have been self-serving and unloving. If he had planned to make a meal that required purchasing very expensive ingredients and following a highly complex recipe that he had never tried, his choice would not have been disobedient but it would have been foolish. The son recognized that he should prepare something that he was capable of doing well that would be enjoyed by the family; out of that loving recognition, he narrowed the options to two choices and then chose one based on that day's weather: it was sunny, a good day for grilling.

Our obedience to God's call is often like that, too. Fundamentally, God calls us to love and serve him in all that we do. Part of "all that we do" includes career. As we seek to obey God in choosing a career, we gradually come to realize what we are capable of doing well and what the needs of our world are. And then we discover that there are three career choices that seem to fit us equally well—we have gifts and passions for them, there's a neediness in the world in these three areas, and each of them is a good place to serve the Lord. In that case, it's as though the Lord says to us, "Go ahead and pick one. You can love and obey and serve me equally well in any one of those three options. Maybe you'll try one and then discover that another choice was better. Go ahead and try. Change your mind later if you need to. I'm with you all the way."

I am currently preparing for my fourth career. Does that mean I got it wrong three times and now finally got it right? Or that I've still got it wrong and hopefully will find the right one (number five) before I retire? I don't think so. I believe God has been with me in each of my careers, using my gifts, leading me on the way, encouraging me to love him in response to his love. I find it wonderfully liberating to be delivered from the anxiety of having to correctly figure out the predetermined; I find that my walk with God has more room for peace and freedom to know that in many areas of my life, there are several obedient options.

I once asked a group of college students this question: "Do you believe that there is only one person out there with whom you can be happily married, or do you believe there are actually several and you are called to discover one of them?" The group unanimously agreed that there are several potential good marriage partners. Their answer also illustrates the "more than one obedient option" principle.

If there are several good options, does that mean that we never make wrong choices? No, we do get it wrong. I have a friend who sensed a call to congregational ministry during his high school years. To pursue that call, he attended four years of college, four years of seminary, and then began work as a pastor. After two years on the job, he realized that he had not heard God's call properly; he resigned from his job and began selling insurance (which he has now done for almost twenty years). He could have entered that profession after two years of study at a community college. Did he waste almost a decade of his life and thousands of tuition dollars because he didn't obey God's call properly? I asked him that question, and I'll never forget his reply: "No, I didn't waste one minute or one dollar. Those years of study strengthened me as a child of God and powerfully shaped me to become the person I am today." We do get it wrong, but God walks with us through our mistakes as well, using them to help us grow as his children. Or, to put it another way, my friend may have answered a question incorrectly in the "What am I supposed to do?" circle, but as he pursued that wrong answer, God strengthened him through the other three circles.

2. God's leading often goes step by step; our focus is daily obedience.

If we think of God as the master planner who has our entire life mapped out, we will focus on trying to understand what our entire life is supposed to look like. But if we think of God as a loving Father who is leading us day by day, shaping us as his disciple-children, we will focus on daily obedience, daily listening, daily faithfulness, daily habits. Jesus teaches, "Seek first his kingdom and his righteousness . . . do not worry about tomorrow, for tomorrow will worry about itself" (Matthew 6:33–34). We are not called to be anxious about the future; we are called to daily faithfulness.

I remember once driving thirty miles through a thick fog late at night. I could see about 20 feet in front of the car; I could see the dotted line on my left and the shoulder of the road on my right. My fear was that a driver in front of me would panic and stop dead on the roadway or that I would unexpectedly come across a stop sign or stoplight. I could have pulled off the road and waited for the fog to lift, but that would have led to a six-hour wait in the middle of the night—not an appealing option. I settled on a speed of about twenty miles an hour, which gave me the confidence to know that I could stay in my lane and stop quickly enough in case something unexpected suddenly came into view.

I find that following God is something like that. He gives us enough guidance to stay in our lane (though sometimes I wish the lines were painted in bolder colors), and, if we take care, we can anticipate most (but not all) unexpected events. We can't see the curves in the road, the corners, or the important landmarks along the way ahead of time, but when it's time to see them, we'll be able to see them. To do that, we

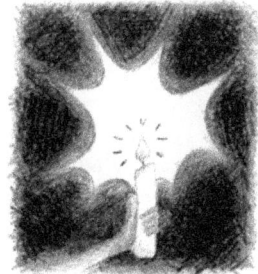

have to keep our foot on the accelerator, our hands on the steering wheel, and our eye on the road. We have to keep on driving to see where the road leads.

An old proverb says, "Life is what happens while you're busy making other plans." The life story of everyone that I know fits with that proverb. I may have had an entire ten-year journey mapped out in my mind, but as I drove through the fog, I discovered that some roads I had planned to take were closed, new ones were open that I wasn't aware of, and the final ten-year destination was not where I was supposed to go! Is that a major disappointment? No, not really. Walking step by step with a faithful God is okay with me. Sometimes it makes me very anxious and I wish that I was the one in control, but deep down I know that he's a better trip planner than I am.

Paul says, "we live by faith, not by sight" (2 Corinthians 5:7). The life lived by faith often appears to be unbearably long and winding: we zig this way and zag that way, learning from our mistakes and plugging along as well as we can. Following God is not *efficient;* it is rarely the shortest distance between two points. I remember once coming to the end of a long road trip; we were forty miles from our destination when we saw the dreaded sign: "Road closed ahead; follow detour." The detour added another twenty miles to the trip, and it was extremely annoying at the end of a long day. Following God is often detour-filled, but—strangely enough—when we look back, we sense that somehow he did not waste our time. Somehow God used all of our experiences to grow us in him. Jayber Crow, the main character in Wendell Berry's novel of the same name, describes this insight as he reflects back on his long life:

> Now I have lived most of the life I am going to have, and I can see what it has been. I can remember those early years when it seemed to me I was cut completely adrift, and times when, looking back at earlier times, it seemed I had been wandering in the dark woods of error. But now it looks to me as though I

was following a path that was laid out for me, unbroken, and maybe even as straight as possible, from one end to the other, and I have this feeling, which never leaves me anymore, that I have been *led*. I will leave you to judge the truth of that for yourself; there is no proof. (*Jayber Crow*, 66, emphasis original)

3. God's leading completely intertwines the present and the future.

During one's younger years, it's tempting to see God's calling as going through a checklist of questions concerning the future. The checklist begins in the junior year of high school: "What do I do after graduation? What college should I attend?" After college begins, we ask, "What major should I register for? Should I get into the 'marriage hunt' or wait awhile?" During the high school or college years, we easily assume that we don't need to think about calling if the right questions have been checked off our list. After finishing college, we assume, issues of calling become more serious as we enter "the real world."

God's leading does not make such a distinction between the present and the future. The "real world," aka, "the kingdom," is not postponed to some distant future. If we limit calling to what we do (especially career-wise), and if college is preparing us for that career, then we will be tempted to perceive calling as a future concern. But if calling focuses on three different pictures— if I am called to hear the celebration and the groaning of creation, to find my niche in the Christian community, and to continue growing as a new creation in Christ—then calling completely intertwines the present and the future.

The Bible frequently compares life *Coram Deo*—life lived before the face of God—to the life of a tree. Psalm 1, for example, says that we are like a tree planted by streams of water when we follow the word of God. I grew up in a fruit belt, an area with millions of fruit trees that produced peaches, pears, apples, plums, cherries, and apricots every year. Imagine a farmer planting a new grove of small fruit trees and saying to himself,

"These trees won't become productive for four years; I can just ignore them until then and concentrate on the rest of my farm."

Ridiculous, we say. Trees that aren't properly nurtured and pruned during their young years will never become strong, mature trees. Proper seasonal care allows them to become what they were meant to be. They may not bear as much fruit during those first years, but their long-term fruit-bearing capacity is greatly shaped by what happens during those early years.

We can look at the relation between the college years and the postcollege years in the same way. Issues concerning life's major decisions—career path, marriage and family, church membership, where to live—may seem somewhat remote. However, growing into the persons that we are called to be is a daily calling that has tremendous bearing upon how we live now and how we will deal with each of those major decisions when the time comes.

Scott figures that someday he'll settle down and get married and be a loving and devoted husband and father, but for now he wants to play the field. He enjoys being around women, having fun, maintaining the reputation of being a ladies' man. Eventually, he realizes that his habits have shaped him to become a certain kind of person, and he can't just push a button and become a different person when he is ready to "settle down."

Marissa came to college from a highly regulated home where almost every minute of the week was scheduled with something or other. She was delighted to discover that in college only seventeen hours of her entire week were scheduled for classes, and the rest of the week was absolutely wide open. She quickly learned that she could stay up until 3 A.M. every day and still concentrate in her 8 A.M. classes, because she had a block free for napping every day from 2–5 P.M. She calculated that her schoolwork could get done between 1–3 A.M., and the rest of the day was pretty much free for whatever happened to come along. Then she found that when 1 A.M. came around, she was often in the middle of very intense discussions, helping friends sort out their personal problems and digging into complex questions about God, the meaning of life, the future, the Bible, and other very important matters. You couldn't just stop these pressing things; loving your neighbor and growing in your faith certainly justified these discussions. Besides, most profs didn't check if the homework was done (much of it seemed optional), and the next test wasn't for three more weeks. Marissa was an honor roll student in her high school, but when her midterm grades came out, she had earned a 2.05 GPA. Basically, Marissa lived a compartmentalized life, associating her coursework with her future calling and everything else about college with the present.

When life is divided into present and future, the present easily takes precedence because the future seems remote, unreal, and less relevant. But if it's true that God's call cannot be compartmentalized into a present and a future, that God is always leading us step by step, forming us as his disciple-children, such compartmentalization becomes a way of blocking out part of God's call in our lives.

4. Obedience involves the whole picture of my life and how it interacts with other lives; in other words, it involves balance.

Living in God's world includes so many wonderful opportunities and, frequently, so many difficult challenges, that it is far too easy to lead an overwhelmed life. There are so many people to get to know, so many activities to become involved in, so many responsibilities that require completion, so many problems that need to be sorted out, and so few waking hours in the day that finding a healthy balance is one of the greatest challenges of them all. This challenge is especially acute during the transition into college because entirely new routines are being established and it takes some time for them to settle into place.

God did not create and redeem us to live as frantic, exhausted people who never do enough for him. We are not called to do absolutely everything that can be done for the Lord; rather, part of our calling is to enjoy Sabbath rest, to receive life as a gift from him. When the prodigal son returned home (Luke 15), he proposed to his father that he be taken back as a hired hand, earning his daily bread. The father would have none of it; he welcomed him home as a son, throwing a huge celebration for the son who was dead and now was alive again. Similarly, our calling includes resting in the Father's love, knowing that he is always at work and therefore we do not need to be.

Dorothy Bass, a wise Christian writer, was once visiting with a group of friends on a Saturday evening, and each one in turn described how busy he or she was going to be the following day. As these descriptions wore on, she suddenly realized that the entire group was taking turns telling how they were planning to break the fourth commandment: "Remember the Sabbath day by keeping it holy . . . on it you shall not do any work" (Exodus 20:8, 10). She began to imagine what it would be like for a group of friends to describe how they planned to worship idols the next day, or commit adultery, or murder. A ridiculous notion, of course. But somehow sharing "I'm too busy" stories did not seem to be a problem. Overcommitment has become the socially acceptable sin of the Christian community.

Because we live in such a frantic, harried culture, learning what *not* to do is often as important as figuring out what we *should* do. The abundant life that Jesus promises in John 10:10 is a life of balance, and through that balance, the light of God's love can shine through us so that the colors of who we are become richer, deeper, and more vibrant.

Habits for Discerning God's Call

Frequently I've heard people say, "I just wish I'd wake up in the morning and find a note under my pillow that said, 'Marry Jon S.' or 'Become a history major' or 'Prepare to become a veterinarian' or 'Move to Alaska.'" Occasionally we hear about people receiving a dramatic sign that pointed them in a clear direction, but most of us go through long and winding processes of discernment as we seek to hear and respond to God's call. There is no simple recipe that we can follow, but there are habits that we can incorporate into our lives that will help the fruit of discernment grow within us.

Habits of listening to the wonder and the groaning of creation

God's work in his world is always so much greater than we can imagine that we need ways of broadening our horizons and expanding the pictures that we see. Habits that help improve our awareness of the wonder and the groaning of creation include:

1. Paying regular attention to global news and finding news sources that do not simply report headlines but also offer in-depth background context and analysis of what is happening.

2. Taking courses that bring us face to face with unfamiliar realities and choosing research topics in our courses that will tune our ears to the beauty and the suffering of God's world.

3. Engaging in volunteer activities that place us in contact with people we do not normally meet. A friend told me that volunteering at the local Family Crisis Center opened her eyes dramatically to the realities that abused women must face (and I've heard many similar stories from others concerning volunteer experiences). Service and mission trips sponsored by churches, Christian organizations, or colleges often provide similar benefits.

Each of these habits or activities has this in common: familiarity tends to deaden our awareness. Experiences that jolt us out of our comfort zones and stretch our horizons help us to see in new ways what God is doing, what the needs of our world are, and what our place there might be.

Habits of listening to the people of God

Often our struggle to discern our calling takes place in private, which is not surprising because our calling is very personal. However, the Lord's statement "it is not good for man to be alone" (Genesis 2:19) applies to the discernment process as well. To understand how God is leading us, we need others. Habits that encourage us to listen to the people of God include:

1. Being as aware as we can of the many creative ways in which believers are seeking first the kingdom. The Christian community is doing so much more than we realize, and our ability to discern God's call is limited by our awareness of the options available to us. Habits that will broaden this awareness include listening to and meeting guest speakers who come to campus, asking professors what activities they are aware of in their areas, and doing web searches for Christian organizations in our field.

2. Asking those who love us and know us well how they see God leading in our lives. Every now and then, a student comes into my office and says, "you've had me in four courses now and know me pretty well. Tell me what my strengths and weaknesses are and where you might see me going after graduation." I have deep admiration for those who make such a request. They are practicing habits of consultation, recognizing that God gave us each other to help us discern his call.

But what if we consult with four people and receive four very different responses? And what if we sense that someone so deeply wants us to move in a particular direction that their advice feels "tainted" by their agenda? Several students have told me that their parents so desperately want them to join a family business or farm that the student didn't feel free to consider whether the Lord might be leading them in a different direction. Such situations illustrate that these habits of discernment are never simple. The advice we receive must itself be discerned: Do these people understand me well? Is this advice driven so deeply by the person's own desires that they are unable to see my life clearly? Am I so driven by my own agenda that I'm not able to properly consider the advice I am given?

Habits of self-reflection

The confusions described in the preceding paragraph remind us that discerning God's call must always include habits of self-reflection as well. God is calling me, he is at work in my life; therefore, I must learn to listen to what is happening inside me. Habits of self-reflection will lead to the following:

1. Recognizing my gifts and abilities. At times, these are obvious, but often they are not. Frequently we are not aware that something we do well can actually be called a gift or ability. For example, our school systems tend to focus on abilities in terms of good grades, athletics, and various kinds of artistic performance (music, drama, and so on). I know someone who does not shine in any of these areas, but in her part-time restaurant job, she is a master at keeping the kitchen organized and calm during the most hectic times. She doesn't think of this as a gift; she figures she's just doing what she's supposed to do. In reality, it's a wonderful gift.

2. Recognizing my passions and desires. Earlier I quoted Frederick Buechner's definition of calling, which invites our deep gladness to meet the world's deep hunger. The phrase *deep gladness* refers to our passions and desires. What is it that makes me burn with excitement, makes me so angry that I desperately want to change something, makes me so sad that I could weep because of the groaning that I hear? It can be difficult to hear our own deep gladness, because we live in a

"whatever" culture: the world is so broken that it hurts too much to care about it, so we are encouraged to shrug our shoulders, say "whatever," and get on with life. But those who are being made new by God may never succumb to a resigned "whatever." Part of our rebirth is that our passions and desires are aligned with the needs of the coming kingdom.

3. Recalling significant memories and life experiences. Remembering the past is crucial for planning for the future. Who are the people you've met about whom you thought, "I'd like to be like her some day"? What situations have led you to conclude, "I could make a difference here"? What have you done that helped you realize, "I'm pretty good at this"?

4. Practicing conversational prayer. Prayer, of course, is a conversation *with* God, not just talking *to* God. We cannot manipulate God into talking to us, but we can learn to become more receptive to listening to him. Prayer that includes times of silence provides opportunities for God's responses to grow in our minds. Prayer journaling may provide opportunity for the Lord to work through our pens as we write. A friend of mine once made a decision that I strongly disagreed with. As her friend, I felt compelled to express my disagreement to her. After listening to me, she said, "Let's both write in a prayer journal about this for a week, and then compare notes." A week later, we discovered that we both agreed about a third option that we hadn't even considered during our first conversation. The prayer journaling brought this new option to light.

5. Remembering that God can lead us anytime, anywhere, in any way. God is the sovereign Lord of the universe, and he can communicate his call to us in millions of different ways. Therefore, we must always be open and alert to receiving his call. One friend who was struggling with a very difficult de-

cision became convinced that a verse on a church sign that she drove by was God's way of pointing her in a particular direction. The advice of others confirmed this leading.

Trying to be open to God's leading in any way can be a dangerous business. I have met people who were convinced that God told them to get married when it was quite obvious that their hormones were talking more loudly than the Lord was. How do we discern the voice of God? Again, there's no recipe, but a life shaped by *many* different habits of discernment—not just one or two—is a life that is in a stronger position to hear God's call.

Habits of courageous risk-taking

Following God's call is almost always scary. One of the most dramatic call stories in Scripture—the call of Moses at the burning bush (Exodus 3–4)—beautifully illustrates how the Lord walks Moses through his reluctant fear. Moses was challenged to practice courageous risk-taking, leaving the relative safety of herding flocks in the wilderness to confront Pharaoh in the name of the Lord. David also left his flocks to take a risk: when young David surprised King Saul by announcing that he, David, would single-handedly attack the enemy giant Goliath, David explained his decision as follows:

> Your servant has killed both the lion and the bear; this uncircumcised Philistine will be like one of them, because he has defied the armies of the living God. The Lord who delivered me from the paw of the lion and the paw of the bear will deliver me from the hand of this Philistine. (1 Samuel 17:36–37)

David could volunteer for his duel with Goliath because he had practiced courageous risk-taking in other difficult situations and had learned that God would be with him.

Risk-taking habits come in hundreds of shapes and sizes. They involve overcoming our natural inclinations and speaking with people we don't normally speak with; participating in events or activities that lie outside our comfort zones; speaking up in classes or peer conversations in ways that may make us nervous but allow us to say what needs to be said; daring to follow the Lord when that conflicts with the expectations of our peer group or our family.

A few years ago, a college student decided to practice courageous risk-taking concerning summer employment. Listen to her story:

We were talking about calling with some friends, discussing the purpose of our summer jobs. I felt at that point that my purpose was simply to go home and make money. I had accepted the job for the second summer in a row and absolutely hated it. I was working as an office manager at an automotive repair shop for a family from our church. It was busy for the first and last hour of the day and I had to "create work" for the other hours of the day. I felt called to work with people, but there wasn't much people-work in this job. The boss was also feeling the stresses of running his own business and was often irritable.

After we discussed risk-taking in class, I decided that I wanted to answer God's call to serve. I especially wanted to serve people instead of making money. I simply trusted that if this was the path God wanted me to take, he would provide. So I set out to volunteer for the summer instead of working. I ended up volunteering at a major cancer hospital. I loved the hospital and took every shift that was available to me there. It was simple work—taking new patients to their appointments and helping them find their way around after arriving at the front desk, pushing patients in wheelchairs, playing with kids and talking with their parents in the waiting rooms, and other little jobs—but I loved it.

It turned out the auto repair shop was desperate for help, so I worked there when I was able. However, I did so with the new approach that I had been forced to think more about: God has called me here for a purpose, even though I

may not like the job. The boss may be stressed and crabby, but God has me here for a reason. In the quiet times up front, I took the opportunity to pray for the guys in the back, crabby boss included. I'm not sure whether more change took place in my heart or his, but I enjoyed the time I spent there that summer and saw God at work daily. God also showed his provision when my grandparents called unexpectedly at the end of the summer and wanted to contribute a little to my tuition because they knew I hadn't been working for money during the summer months. It was a simple (and yet overwhelming at the time) reminder that he was taking care of me.

It taught me a lot. It was an opportunity to trust that God blesses obedience. I know that my parents were not very pleased about my decision to volunteer during the summer and still think it feasible to finance college tuition in the fall. Yet I wanted my heart to be in the right place, and I felt that volunteering allowed me to ensure that I was serving for the right reasons. I learned a lot and was blessed by the opportunities I had. God still put me back at the auto shop, but in the meantime he worked on my heart and my attitude to make it useful for serving him.

All of these habits not only support us in answering the question, "What is God calling me to do?" but they also support us as we are becoming new creations in Christ. About twenty years ago, I heard a speaker conclude a presentation with a simple devotional poem entitled "The Road of Life." Since then, that poem has hung on my office wall, reminding me what it means to follow God by practicing habits of discernment.

The Road of Life

At first, I saw God as my observer, my judge,
keeping track of things I did wrong,
so as to know whether I merited heaven or hell when I die.
He was out there sort of like a president.
I recognized his picture when I saw it,
but really didn't know Him.

But later on
when I met Christ,
it seemed as though life were rather like a bike ride,
but it was a tandem bike,
and I noticed that Christ
was in the back helping me pedal.

I don't know just when it was
that He suggested we change places,
but life has not been the same since.

When I had control,
I knew the way.
It was rather boring,
but predictable . . .
It was the shortest distance between two points.

But when he took the lead,
He knew delightful long cuts,
up mountains,
and through rocky places
at breakneck speeds;
it was all I could do to hang on!
Even though it looked like madness,
He said, "Pedal!"

I worried and was anxious
and asked,
"Where are you taking me?"
He laughed and didn't answer,
and I started to learn trust.

I forgot my boring life
and entered into the adventure.
And when I'd say, "I'm scared,"
He'd lean back and touch my hand.

He took me to people with gifts that I needed,
gifts of healing,
acceptance

and joy.
They gave me gifts to take on my journey,
My Lord's and mine.

And we were off again;
He said, "Give the gifts away;
they're extra baggage, too much weight."
So I did,
to the people we met,
and I found that in giving, I received,
and still our burden was light.
I did not trust Him,
at first,
in control of my life.
I thought He'd wreck it;
but He knows bike secrets,
knows how to make it bend to take sharp corners,
knows how to jump to clear high rocks,
knows how to fly to shorten scary passages.

And I am learning to shut up
and pedal
in the strangest places,
and I'm beginning to enjoy the view
and the cool breeze on my face
with my delightful constant companion, Jesus Christ.

And when I'm sure I just can't do anymore,
He just smiles and says, "Pedal."

Jim Hansel, in *Holy Sweat*

Epilogue

A Story of Seeking

First the Kingdom

Note: Everything in the story that follows is based on actual people and actual events, with enough details changed to keep everyone anonymous.

Jennifer had dreamed all of her life about getting married and having many children. She married Rob, her childhood sweetheart, when she turned twenty, and by the time she was thirty, they had five children. But long before that, she knew that things weren't going the way she had dreamed. Rob had no patience with the children. He easily flew into a rage when they were too demanding or cried too much. When Michael, their oldest, was four, Rob slammed him so hard into the wall that he broke his arm. Jennifer took Michael to the hospital and made up a story about him falling off his bike.

Five years later, she had to do it again. This time it was Katie's arm; Jennifer lied again, telling a story about Katie slipping on the ice on the front steps, but she knew that it was time to make a drastic change. She called the family crisis center in town, and the next day, when Rob was at work, she kept the kids home from school, packed up the minivan full of their clothes and favorite toys, and drove the whole troop over to the crisis center.

Amy was the social worker on duty that morning. After they both got the kids settled in the facility's playroom, Amy sat down to talk with Jennifer.

"So why did you lie about Katie's broken arm?" Amy asked.

"I wasn't ready to have the police involved and to press

charges," replied Jennifer. "It was too scary and would lead to too much chaos. But I knew that for the sake of the kids I couldn't stay."

"Well, the police will have to be involved now. And we'll need to talk with a lawyer and also set up an appointment for you with the welfare office."

Jennifer sat silently in a state of semishock. Welfare? All her life, her church had told her that welfare was for lazy ne'er-do-wells, parasites of the state. A lawyer? She had made a public vow to be faithful to Rob for the rest of her life. Could she now say things that could well result in a prison sentence for him? She had hoped that by leaving home she would shock Rob into changing and that now he would welcome the family home on his knees, promising to become a new man for the rest of his life. Was it too late for that?

She asked Amy that question. Amy shook her head sadly. "Two things you need to know," she replied. "First, by law I am required to report what has happened to Katie. Rob's actions constitute a criminal act against a child, and I am a mandatory reporter. Second, I would guess that this is not the first time something like that has occurred in your home, and he's probably gone after you, too—am I right? "

Despairingly, Jennifer nodded slowly. "I can't count the times," she whispered, "the vast majority of them didn't require medical attention."

"Most violent men are not willing to change. And those who are only do so with significant help and time."

"But I can't afford a lawyer," said Jennifer, "I can't even afford to feed my kids tonight."

"Don't worry about money right now," replied Amy, "The same group of churches that supports this center provides legal services to those who need it. I'll set up an appointment for you this afternoon."

"Lots of times I've thrown a dollar into the collection plate to support this place," reflected Jennifer, "but I never thought I'd be sitting here making use of that offering."

"Well, you sure aren't the first church-goer to come here. Nationally, domestic abuse is just as prevalent among Christians as it is among the rest of the population."

Amy noticed that Jennifer looked shocked. "You lied about your kids' injuries, right? Believe me, there are a million more lies like those. "

Later that afternoon, Brady, a young lawyer in town, stopped by the center. Jennifer couldn't contain her curiosity. "So why do you come here? You could be making bigger bucks working out business contracts, settling estates, and closing real estate deals."

"I do all of that too, but this week I'm on call for the center. I've always had a passion for justice in the home, and I serve as a consultant on a state committee that is examining how the state responds to domestic problems. There are days when the more I hear about the problems, the more I want to run and hide my head inside 900-page business contracts, but then I remember that I've been blessed with the ability to make a difference and I keep at it."

"Why are you so passionate? Did you grow up in a messed-up home?"

"No, it started in college. I went on a weeklong service project and met a lawyer who worked in an inner city. I was a business major at the time, and, after meeting her, I kept my major and worked towards a prelaw emphasis as well. I've kept in touch with her over the years, and she continues to be my inspiration, my mentor."

The matters that had to be dealt with that day were sorted out, Jennifer and her children were settled in, and Amy headed out to her home, fifteen miles west and two towns up the highway. She relished that drive home every afternoon: a quiet car, one cigarette that usually lasted about six miles, the sun shining on rolling hills teeming with corn and beans. She always felt as though she was privileged to glimpse the grandeur of God as she digested the brokenness and groaning of creatures made in his image. She often found herself praying on the way home with words like, "Shine, Jesus, shine, fill this land with the Father's glory," or "Lord, take these twisted lives and do your straightening work in ways that are too much for me to do," or "Lord, take my own struggling life and give me the courage and perseverance to hang in there with you."

As Amy drove away from Jennifer dealing with Katie's broken arm and all the rest, she found herself worrying about her son Brandon, sixteen, school basketball star. "Good kid," she thought, "but why is he so obsessed with sports, cars, and girls? I wish he would hear Jennifer's story firsthand and see Katie. I wish he would see Brady in action and catch a bit of Brady's passion. I wish . . ."

The clouds off to the left caught her eye. Their coloring through the filtered sunlight was beautiful beyond description, filled with shades of white and gray tinged by orangy purple. "Ok, Lord, it's in your hands. You are on your throne and your kingdom is coming, even though things look and feel so messy down here much of the time. Fill me with your Spirit so that I will trust you more fully, and cleanse my eyes to see your kingdom coming in me, around me, and all over this beautiful but broken world that you love so much that you gave your only son for it. Amen."

She hoped that Brandon had remembered to take the steaks out of the freezer for her husband to grill.